DATE DUE

GAYLORD   PRINTED IN U.S.A.

GOLDEN GATE SEMINARY LIBRARY

NO EXCUSES ACCEPTED

ROBERT GILBERT
with Nancy B. Barcus

BROADMAN PRESS
Nashville, Tennessee

© Copyright 1988 • Broadman Press
All Rights Reserved
4250-55
ISBN: 0-8054-5055-6
Dewey Decimal Classification: B
Subject Heading: GILBERT, ROBERT // HANDICAPPED, BIOGRAPHY
Library of Congress Catalog Number: 87-24221
Printed in the United States of America

Library of Congress Cataloging-in-Publication Data

Gilbert, Robert, 1932-
  No excuses accepted.

  1. Christian life—Baptist authors.   2. Gilbert,
Robert, 1932-   . I. Barcus, Nancy B. II. Title.
BV4501.2.G487 1988   248.4'86132   87-24221
ISBN 0-8054-5055-6 (pbk.)

*To my wife Elwayne
and my sons
Ja Ja and Kenyatta*

Contents

1. God Says, "You Can!" 9
2. No Excuses: God Is More than Sufficient 19
3. You're Never Too Ill for God 33
4. Depression: God Can Heal Our Minds 49
5. Poverty: Blessing in Disguise 67
6. Stress: It Brings Out the Tough Side of Faith 79
7. Rejection: God Honors Our Courage 95
8. His Eye Is on the Sparrow: And I Know He Watches Me 115

1
God Says, "You Can!"

God says, "You *can!*" God says you can do anything. There is nothing on this earth strong enough to hold you back from what you can do for Him. I know that, because my life has tested the limits of God's strength and power. I want to tell everyone who is feeling discouraged for any reason that God is stronger than their most serious problem. Whatever He has put in your heart to do—you can do it!

I can say this because for the last thirty years I have suffered from a form of arthritis that has gradually fused every joint in my body. Today it is difficult for me to walk. I cannot turn my head to the right or the left. I wake up in great pain every morning of my life. I have to be lifted and carried to my destination every time I go out of the house. But none of that has stopped God from using my life to serve Him. I see God at work in my life more powerfully than ever before. I see people coming to God and committing their lives to Him as I testify to His power and grace. I want to tell everyone what God can do for them. He can do anything for you that you need.

I know that because I have seen His strength within me increase as my body has weakened. I have been near death many times, given up in despair by doctors and by my family. I have been hospitalized more than forty times and have endured heart surgery, abdominal surgery, bone and joint surgery, and health conditions that made people think I would be hopeless and helpless if I lived. Through all those times, I *knew* God would bring me through. When I was too weak to pray, others prayed for me because they shared my belief in the goodness and sufficiency of our God. They knew that God had given me a testimony to the greatness of His mercy and we determined together to let His praise be known.

People who meet me for the first time see only the thin frame of my body, and perhaps they notice my hands, bent back at the wrists from the arthritis so I can barely use them. Perhaps they notice the scaling of my skin, caused by an uncomfortable side effect of my illness. But I watch their eyes as we begin to talk, or as I begin to preach God's Word to them. I see them forgetting everything about me but what we are sharing together about God. I see them eager to hear what God can do for them. In their faces I see the hunger to believe that if God can sustain me, then He can sustain them, too.

If God can use my pain and my frailty to convince others of His power, what more can I ask? There was a time when I wanted to give up. I said to the Lord that if I could no longer walk, life would not be worth living. I said that I did not want to be dependent on others, as my arthritis has caused me to be. But God said, "My strength is made perfect in weakness" (2 Cor. 12:9). He showed me that "I can do all things through Christ," who strengthens me (Phil. 4:13). I decided to believe His promise that He can do so much more than we "ask or think" (Eph. 3:20). And I have found Him faithful beyond anything I imagined.

In my church on Sunday mornings, I watch the faces of my congregation. Carver Park Baptist Church in East Waco has grown from sixty to three-hundred members since the church called me as pastor in 1978. I said to them once, "You know my condition," and they called me anyway. They wanted to hear my testimony of the power of God to sustain our lives together. As they believed God and saw Him work, their giving has increased and the church has prospered. As I have endured illness and pain, they have stood with me, believing God for me and keeping the church programs and services going during my times of illness. They are an unusual church. They have vowed to stand with me and they have never left my side when I needed them. Their prayers and our worship together have strengthened us all.

Today, when they bring me into the service and set me in my chair, or roll my chair into position where I can see all their faces, I see their eyes brighten in anticipation. I feel the Spirit of God lifting me up at the beginning of our services together. The presence of God among us during those services makes me marvel at what God can do. God only asks for lives given over to Him. He only requires our willingness to serve. He can do all the rest. I know that beyond the shadow of a doubt. So do the people I love in this church. God has done great things among us. He meets our needs, not because we are strong, but because He is.

There is no doubt in my mind. If God says, "You can," then you can. You can do anything He calls you to do. No physical or mental problems can stop God from having His way in your life. Ask Him, and you will see.

When I meet someone who doubts God's power or who thinks God has given up on them, I want to tell them my story. I want to tell them how much I have endured and how much God has held me up. I want to tell them that it is not just illness that God can overcome. He can overcome personal problems, marriage problems, depression, despair, rejection, foolish mistakes, poverty, and every other kind of weakness. I know that because God has delivered me from all those things. I have survived depression, discouragement, rejection of my efforts to be a community leader, early childhood poverty, interruptions of my education, misunderstandings within my family, and problems with my children. Through all these testings, I have discovered that there is no problem too difficult for God.

If you think you have to be strong, outstanding, and already perfect before God can use you, I have a better testimony. The only thing God ever required of me was to be willing to serve Him. Every time I listened to His leading in my life, He did the rest. When I ignored His pull upon my life, I met with disaster. God never meant for us to walk this life alone. If we have problems, they are there to remind us how much we need God. Only through His power and love does our life have any meaning. Walk away from God for even a day, and you will see how empty you are. We were meant to live with Him and to live for Him. As long as we are doing that, everything else is possible.

I spent some years of my life running from God. I was raised to know Him and to believe in Him. But I am a stubborn and independent person, and I wanted to stand on my own. I made some mistakes. I suffered for them. Others suffered for them, too. When I became ill, I blamed God in my bitterness. I felt myself drifting farther and farther from hope and from healing. My independence and fighting spirit had come to nothing.

I am thankful that friends and family prayed for me. I believe the greatest gift God can give us is someone to pray for us. My father, who was a minister all his adult life, never stopped praying for me. So did others in my family who saw me suffer the consequences of my bad decisions and the pain of my increasing illness. I felt God pulling on my life, even as I was determined to make my way through all my troubles without Him. I finally stopped resisting His claim upon me and I told Him I would trust Him and serve Him. The stress caused by my problems began to ease. My bitterness left me. My life gradually began to make sense. My strength to live a productive life returned. I saw, even as I see now, that only when we give ourselves wholly to God does life have any meaning at all.

Since that first time of surrender, I have surrendered many times to the claim of God upon my life. Whenever I am tempted to despair, I remember what He has done for me. I remember how He has given me hope when I had none. I remember how He has brought me healing when the doctors despaired. I remember how He has lifted me up to praise Him when I had no joy in my heart.

When we are most discouraged and cast down, God is not far away. He can place within our hearts the longing to return to Him. He can give us the grace to lay down our stubborn wills and come to His better will. He can supply the answers to our nagging questions that keep us from His side. He can supply prayer support from others who care for us when we feel the most alone in our weakness. All these things and more He can and will do for us because He loves us.

I know that, because God has proved Himself in my life. I will spend the rest of my days saying what He has done for me—because I know He can do it for anyone. I know He can do it for you.

Every day we find some new way to discover God's mercy in our lives. If I am at home and in pain or in need of being lifted up, someone comes to me to say they are praying. Or someone tells me later they were praying. I can't think of a single dark day in my life when God did not give me some sign that He knew of my condition and was at work to change and to heal. I need only to be alert for the signs of his mercy to see them. I think we miss those signs on the days we fail to believe in Him. On those days everything seems dark, and we aren't even looking for His support and strength. I know how much of His mercy we miss because we fail to look for it. We need to be aware of his tender kindness.

I remember a day when I was very low and discouraged. It was a time when I had begun to believe God had abandoned me. Others had to tell me where to look to find God's grace. These were the circumstances: I had been rushed to the best heart specialists in the nation for open-heart surgery in early fall 1984. The doctors were confident about the surgery, but they felt I was a poor risk because of my skin condition and because the infection found in my heart was often fatal. On the way to Houston for the surgery, I had a slight stroke and did not recognize anybody for several hours. My family believed my life and ministry were over when this happened. But prayer followed me and God held me up to survive the surgery. I received a new heart valve and a pacemaker. We all regarded my survival as a special mercy from the Lord, and I know of so many who prayed and fasted for me. After this, my recovery was a matter of time and everyone continued confident at my upward progress.

But I began to be impatient and to despair of ever getting on my feet again. What is more, a fever began to attack my body as I lay at home waiting to be well. After all God had done to sustain me through the surgery, I began to feel I was finished after all. My spirits sank. I had lost the muscle tone in my legs, I discovered, as I tried to walk about on crutches. After a few weeks back in my church and a brief feeling of hope around Thanksgiving, I began to sink down again and decided God was through using me. Two of my closest friends died, and my pain and fever soared. The doctors were puzzled at what was going wrong with my body. They ran tests and came to no definite conclusions.

"It happens sometimes with your kind of arthritis," they said. "Maybe it's a return of the heart infection," they said. "We'll have to do more surgery, if it is." They even asked me if I wanted to be kept alive artificially, if my health deteriorated that far. I said no, that God Himself must take me at His own time. More surgery would mean death, I was sure. *Perhaps it was my time,* I thought.

I should have known better. All the signs in my life so far had been that God had more for me. I had two young sons, Ja Ja, twelve, and Kenyatta, ten. I needed to see them grow to spiritual maturity and they needed my strong hand because they are a handful for my wife to manage by herself. God had given me, too, a dream for Carver Park Church. Often when I am ill, God uses that time to show me what else He would have me to do. I had come out of my heart surgery with a clear vision of what I wanted to see happening in that church. These ambitions from the Lord should have been enough to remind me that He would sustain me. I should have realized that He doesn't give us dreams or clear callings to action only to frustrate us. If He gives us a calling, He will see that we fulfill it.

I have learned so often over the years that when we are too weak to pray, others are not. My brother Sam called from his church in Houston. He and his church of a thousand members were praying, he said. My church was praying, too. My lifelong friend sat by my bed and prayed with me for the first time in all the years we had known each other. My sister reminded me of my father's words to us in childhood about "putting feet on our prayers" through fasting. A friend asked a prayer partner to fast and pray, and Carver Park Church asked to join them in that vigil. Rev. Joe Montgomery on the radio asked for others to join in that meeting. Others also prayed and later told me of it. As they prayed, I lay on my bed, hurting too much even to think.

The next day the fever was better, then worse again. I wondered if the prayers were working.

"Believe God before He answers," my friends told me.

"I see the answer, even if you don't feel it yet," a longtime friend told me.

My wife needed this answer as much as I did. She was very weary and discouraged with caring for me in this desperate condition for so long. For nearly nine months I had been in bed with little sign of improvement.

My brother called me from Houston to see if I felt the encouragement of God's spirit yet. I needed help, I told him.

"You need to 'eat' God's Word," he said. "When you feel as discouraged as you are now, you need to actively do something to help yourself."

He gave me some verses to read and I promised I would spend some time praying over them. I know today, as a result of his encouragement, that the lowest time in our spiritual journey is the time we most need to take action. That is always the time we least feel like it. But action is urgent and imperative. If we don't take hold of God's Word at times like these, we hinder God from helping us.

That night I had a dream which also showed me this. I was at my childhood home, sitting with my family at an outdoor picnic table. My mother passed a plate of meat loaf, and when it came to me, I cut into it, and the meat became a black Bible. I put the Bible on my plate and began pulling pages out and eating them. When I woke up I began to meditate on the verses my brother had recommended to me.

"We have this treasure in earthen vessels, that the excellency of the power may be of God, and not of us," I read in 2 Corinthians 4:7. "Be strong and of a good courage," said Joshua (1:9).

"Bless the Lord, O my soul, and forget not all his benefits," Psalm 103:2 urged me.

Then Romans 8:35 reminded me that nothing in heaven or earth could separate me from the love of Christ.

I let those words sift through my mind and then I focused upon them. I realized again that the excellency of the power of God is far beyond our understanding. Our life does not depend on our power, but only on His power. We are promised that this Power is there to lift us from every circumstance. Our only job is to strengthen ourselves in courage. That is what Joshua was commanded—to have courage. God did all the rest. We may be weak from our many problems and burdens, but we can have courage even when we have nothing else.

God-given courage is based on two things: The first is our memory of everything else God has done for us in the past to lead us forward. We need to recount His blessings. We need to think back in our own history to all the times He has met us and helped us and given us what we needed. How quickly we forget all his benefits once the next problem comes to us! The Bible says in Psalm 103:2, "Bless the Lord," and "forget not all his benefits"! We can bless God, no matter what is presently happening to us. We can remember all He has done!

The second basis for our courage is a belief that God has all power in heaven and earth—for the future as well as the past. As far as the future is concerned, the Bible says "nothing can separate us from the love of Christ." We may feel that everything around us is in shambles. We may feel that we have no strength and no inner resources to lift ourselves up. But God has "all power . . . in heaven and in earth" (Matt. 28:19), and He has an unbreakable promise that nothing—the word is *nothing*—shall separate us from the love of Christ. Not today. Not tomorrow.

He loves us. His love is always present, always available, always surrounding us, whether we are aware of it or not. We may not feel it. Our hearts may be numb, dry, or hurting with great sorrow and pain. But His love is there, even if we don't feel it. His love has been there since the beginning of time. There's a song that says that long before I knew my own name, God loved me. God's love stands behind us from the very beginning.

As I let these thoughts sink into my mind, I felt a gradual cooling come to me. My pain dropped to where I could be propped up for the first time in many days.

I began to dress again, to go out, to take over the services in my church. Finally, I preached one Sunday morning. I even visited the hospital to call on sick church members. A nurse stopped me and said, "We never thought we would see you again, you were so sick. And here you are, calling on sick people!"

I told her God had delivered me. I saw her smile at the thought.

"He can do anything," I said. "I'm here to tell you that."

For the rest of my life I want to give glory to God for what He has done. I believe that is why He has sustained my life. I can tell anyone, no matter how far down they feel, that God is capable of everything. He holds the key to everything we need. We should never say we can't do something when God says we can. Whatever it is, God says we can do it. He is able, far beyond anything we can understand. We must wait upon Him.

2
No Excuses: God Is More than Sufficient

People say I'm too hard on them. I'm hard on myself, too. That's because God gives me the strength to be hard on myself. I believe He gives all of us the strength to be hard on ourselves. We mustn't expect anything except His very best in our lives because He wants to give us everything we need. I can't understand anyone who wants less than the best God has for them.

I spend my life pleading with people to accept from God's hand what He has promised. It frustrates me to see people who don't even ask God for what they need the most. I believe God has something very special for every person alive. I have pleaded with the people in Carver Park Baptist Church to see that and to accept God's will in their lives.

I know how much God has for them because He has given so much to me. In my own strength, I have so little to boast of. Anyone looking at me can see how little strength I have. I don't have beauty, a fine physique, wealth, or any of those things so many people think they must have in order to be happy. God has shown me that you don't need all those things. There was a time when I had more strength and more of life's other benefits, but those weren't always the times when I felt closest to God or truly at peace. I can say today that none of those things matters or makes any difference at all. God may choose to give them to you. He may take them away. They mean nothing. Only God's peace within you can do anything to make you happy.

I don't like to hear people make excuses for why they aren't happy. I know what it is to suffer, so I am very sympathetic with every kind of suffering and pain. I understand how much life can hurt, too. But even when life was hurting me the most, I learned not to use that as an occasion to avoid God. When I let bitterness overwhelm me, God was not able to move toward me and help me. When I used my troubles as an excuse for why I was not close to God, I thwarted His wonderful intentions for my life. He wanted to show me His power even in my times of greatest weakness. Feeling bitter, making excuses, or letting anger at other people cloud our lives—all these things prevent God from moving toward us with all His grace, power, and love.

I've learned not to give God any excuse for anything. All He asks is that we be committed to His working in our lives. He will do all the rest.

Commitment means coming to God just as we are—no matter what is bothering us and no matter what seems to be standing in the way of our peace of mind. Commitment is telling God that we give everything over to Him to do with us whatever He will. Commitment is believing that God has heard us and then simply waiting for Him to do His work in our lives. When we are committed, we hang on to God's promises in the present moment and refuse to be swayed by our changing feelings or circumstances. We have told God we believe Him, and we must not go back on that contract. Commitment to God operates the same way love operates. When you are committed to someone you love, you refuse to let anything change that agreement to stand together. In just that way, God is committed to us in every circumstance, and He only waits for us to display the same commitment toward Him.

Today when I awake in the mornings, I could be tempted to say to God that I am hurting too much or feeling too weak to let Him use me this day. I could be tempted to say that I am not satisfied with the life He has given me. But I know from experience that as soon as I do, that I cut God off from working in my life. I close up the channel of communication and love which He exercises toward me. Instead, I have learned to begin the day by praying for His work and will in my life. And I have learned to wait upon Him to see what He will do that day.

Gradually, as I wait prayerfully upon Him, I come to a positive view of the day. I find my pain easing enough so that I can do whatever He has set before me. I find hope and meaning in the thought that He has renewed me once more. If I had chosen to let despair overwhelm me, I would have cut myself off from all the love and support God offers through His spirit. If I had decided not to be open to God today, I would have missed His newest blessing upon my life.

I've spent some of my days keeping God at a distance. I know what it is to refuse to let Him come close. I know the dryness and discouragement of those days. I've learned the hard way that the only good day is a day when God is near. I long for those days now, and do everything in my power to assure that I am receptive to His grace. I don't want to be far from God in my spirit. I'm only happy and useful when I have allowed Him to come close.

I've discovered that our usefulness does not depend on our strength, but on God's strength. I know that, because when I stopped making excuses about my weakness, God used me in spite of my weakness.

On days when I feel tired and unable to do all I want to do, I still find God somehow making a way for me. People come to me to pour out their problems. They are healthy people, strong people, but people with hurt and separation on the inside of their lives. When they come, I have to put away every thought of weakness or tiredness that I may feel and give myself over to God's strength, so I can help them. We talk together, pray together, and I feel Him sustaining me in some unusual way far beyond my own human power and health. God ministers between us, bringing hope to these people as we talk and bringing strength to my body. I've found that opening myself up to the presence of God's Spirit makes everything possible.

People ask me sometimes how I do it. They come to me at home on a day when my pain is intense, and they wonder if they could do what I do. I'm often lying down to conserve my strength, and I see in their eyes that they are glad not to be in my condition. But as we begin to talk about whatever they came for, I forget my pain and become drawn into their conversation. I see them forgetting their thoughts about me and asking me for advice and counsel. As I see them pouring out their concerns to me, I realize that they are no longer thinking of me as a weak person. They are regarding me as someone strong enough to help them find the way. Afterwards, when I think about it, I realize that God's definition of strength and weakness is completely different from ours. Weakness is not what you can see. Weakness is on the inside where we've failed to let God take hold of us. Strength is not something you can see. Strength is on the inside, where our weakness is made perfect in God's strength. When the Spirit of God takes hold of us right where we are, things happen for us and for other people that would never otherwise have been possible. I have experienced that so many times.

Some days, I wonder if I can possibly preach or lead in a service. I begin to pray for God's strength. At those times, every joint in my body aches, and sometimes a mild fever which is part of my arthritis races through my body, parching my throat and my skin. I wonder if I can sit up, let alone conduct a service before more than two-hundred people in a church service. Even on those days, except for some exceptional times when I have to rest longer before I can move and function enough to be out of the house, I feel something happening to me as I enter the church building. No matter how much pain I have felt while my family and another adult who helps us have struggled to move me and get me ready, I feel strength enter into me as the service begins. I've been lifted out of the car, and my boys have steadied my feet as I sit in my chair. They put my Bible and papers in my hands, and one of my faithful deacons from the church comes to take me into the service. I enter, praying within me and waiting upon God. Before me are all the expectant faces of the people who have come to God's house once more to find His renewing touch. They are weary, tired, distressed with one another, in financial trouble, and discouraged about their families. I look into their faces and see how much they need the touch of God in their lives. And I ask God for the strength to minister that touch to them through His Spirit. I cannot disappoint them.

God never fails me. His Spirit lifts me up almost at the moment the service begins. I feel myself sitting up straighter, as if heavenly hands have made me firm. I feel God giving me words to speak, prayers to offer on their behalf, and a gentleness and love toward all who have come. As we begin to sing some of the many hymns and songs that point us to God's mercy, my mind becomes clear with the words I want to share with them. All through the service, His Spirit hovers close, and I feel the renewing of His presence coming to so many. I can see in the faces of those who are singing that they are thinking of God's love. I can see the relief come to some of the tired faces. At midweek services I thank God for the women who have been working all day and barely arriving home in time to feed their families before coming; for the men who faithfully come to the services even when something is bothering them from a long and burdensome day. I know that no matter how weary any of us feels, God will not disappoint us. He has enough in His storehouse for everyone who has come.

I often look at the young people who come out to the services and who sing in the choir. I'm glad their families are seeing to it that they come to church. I believe that only through God's grace can their dreams and promises be fulfilled. I know it is tempting for young people to look for their dreams somewhere else besides in God. They haven't tripped over all the bumps and hard things in life yet, and some of them don't know what lies ahead. They don't know how much they will need God's resources within them. They think that success on the basketball court or in the beauty pageant will take them a long way. How little they know of what life will require of them. When they stumble, they need to know God is there. I don't want them *ever* to think that the hard times which come to them have the power to keep them away from God. I don't want them to use those hard times as an excuse to avoid God. God doesn't need any excuses from us, no matter what happens. He wants to give us all of Himself and He wants our total trust, in good times and in bad. In return, He never fails us. God doesn't require that we must be perfect before we trust Him. He only asks that we never stop trusting in Him.

I know this so well myself that I want to do everything in my power to prevent others—especially young people and young families—from making excuses that will keep them away from God. No excuse is a good excuse. When God wants so much for us, we dare not deny Him the opportunity to do His work within our lives.

Nothing pains me more than to see young people with so much potential making excuses that keep God from working. I wonder how much more He could have done with me if I had given Him everything in my life much sooner. I'll never know the answer to that. All I know is that these people in our church have so much to look forward to from His grace if they will give God the chance to work.

The people in our church are suffering from difficult marriages. They are worried about children who are in trouble at school or after school. They are frustrated because they aren't advancing in their jobs. They feel passed over and stuck in a rut. They are angry with one another because they can't agree in committee meetings or their mission groups about how they want to do things. They wish one or another of their members would leave, so everything would be easier for them. Or they wish people would accept their solutions to certain problems, instead of arguing so much about the best way to do something. And they let those things get them down. They think God can't work in their lives or in the church because they keep stumbling into so much daily stress and trouble. They begin to pray for solutions for these problems and to hold it against God if He doesn't answer their prayers their way. They haven't even given Him a chance when they do that. So they become angry and frustrated at God for not responding according to their plan.

Yes, we all ask God for specific answers to problems sometimes. That's a good thing to do, but not if we are using those prayers as a test of God's reality. We say, "God, if You can solve this problem, then maybe I'll really believe what

You are able to do." But sometimes we don't mean that prayer at all. We just want some burden to be lifted, so we can go on with our lives the way they already are. We don't really want to be changed or taken over by God. We don't really want to be renewed in His Spirit so that everything that happens to us is under His control.

I wonder sometimes why more of my people have not entered into the fullness of life that Christ intends. I grieve sometimes for the people in the church who seem to be standing just at the doorway of God's purposes, but they never enter. I can't understand anymore what keeps someone from asking God for everything He has for their lives. His way is the way of joy. It is so much better than anything we can ever do for ourselves.

People tell me they are seeking joy; they are seeking peace; they are seeking rest. I want to say, "Well, it is yours then. Take it." I feel that they don't really have it because they haven't made that 100-percent transaction with God to bring His joy into their lives.

God wants so much more from us. Of course, He will never force Himself upon us. He didn't force His way into my life. He just kept waiting until I recognized that none of my problems were so big that He couldn't work in my life anyhow.

All my sermons, since my last illness and heart surgery, have been pointed toward this need for commitment. I know that no one in my church can be happy—with themselves, with their families, or with each other—unless they have taken this step of trust. Fifty-percent Christianity is not enough. God cannot do with us what He wants to do unless He has all of our hearts.

I have a sermon: "God wants more from you." I tell my congregation, "You say to me that I expect too much from you. I admit that I do. But it's not Robert Gilbert who expects it. It's God. He wants so much more for you.

"I'm not saying that what I'm asking you to do is easy. I am saying that it is the only road to true life, true peace, and rest from all the problems that we bring on ourselves by holding back from letting God take them.

"We are content to bargain with God over first one problem and then another, all the while holding ourselves back from making the complete bargain with Him for our lives.

"Our prayers will never really produce God's results that way. Yes, He may choose to answer some request of ours. But what He is really waiting for us to do is to make a full commitment of our lives first. God wants 100 percent of us. He wants our hearts. He wants our wills. He wants our talents. He wants our love for Him before everything else. If we give Him our lives, He will do all the rest. If we could only see that no excuse is sufficient to keep Him from doing His work, we would stop wasting His time and ours and accept everything He has for us.

"I look at myself sometimes. I want to get up and walk again, or even just stand on crutches to preach this sermon. I want to get rid of all my pain.

"But then I remember that Paul had a health problem, too. He called it his 'thorn in the flesh' (2 Cor. 12:7). We don't really know what it was, but it was always there. Paul prayed three times to be free of his 'thorn'. He didn't like to think that it would hold him back from doing all he needed to do.

"God came to him and said, 'My grace is sufficient for you.' I want to tell you His grace is sufficient for you and for me, too. The grace God has for us is always adequate and enough. We must never say 'I can't' about anything to God."

When I preach that sermon, I hear some of my people

beginning to speak out to God in prayer. I hear them saying, "Yes, Lord." When I hear them responding to the Spirit in that way, I want to give them some extra encouragement.

I have a song I like to sing. I often sing it or some other favorite at the end of my services. One thing I have never lost through all my illnesses is my voice. It is the voice of a strong man, and when I sing, people look at me in surprise the first time they hear me. I can sing sitting down, even though my arthritis has affected the way I breathe. The sound resonates and my words come out clear and loud. My songs are part of my sermon. I sing that I don't feel "no ways tired," that the road is not easy, but that I *know* He'll go with me all the way.

I look out at my congregation. They are clapping and nodding as I finish the song. I see some tears. I feel the Spirit take the message into several hearts. I see a recently baptized girl smiling and tapping her foot. I pray for her to understand how much God has for her in the life which lies ahead of her.

At the end of the service I watch the people get up to leave, talking, looking quiet and serious, or sometimes seeming to have heard nothing. I watch for a moment a woman I know who has been having a serious argument with another woman in this church. I wonder if she heard me today.

I see someone else welcoming a visitor to the church, and I hear snatches of their conversation as others come up and begin to talk with me. I hear the woman in my church say, "I never complain about my life after I've heard Rev. Gilbert."

"He's an inspiration." I hear the visitor say. I want to go over to them and say it is God who is the inspiration. I hope they understand that. Then I am thankful if in some small way this wretched life of mine can be used to show God's

No Excuses: God Is More than Sufficient 29

mercy. Whatever pain I feel, everything is worth it if I have helped someone else to claim God's promises.

My son Ja Ja comes over to me and pleads with me to go home. His face is soft for a moment, and he tickles my ear. "Come on," he says. I tell him I must stay a few more minutes and talk to the people. They want to come up to me and tell me what is bothering them. And I find myself offering more words of encouragement to them from God's Word. There seems no end to the troubles that come to people, but I know there is no end to God's answers for them, either. I want to stay with the people after the service for as long as they need me, even though I am feeling very tired now.

Finally, one of the deacons takes hold of my chair and rolls me toward the door. Ja Ja and Kenyatta run along beside me. My wife has driven the car right up to the door and is waiting for me.

I look at her. If there is anyone who could make excuses, it is she—my wife of twenty years. She knew of my precarious health when she married me, but I was walking back then, even though I had some pain. Her family opposed the idea of her marriage to me, but she insisted and she has stayed firm in her resolve. She's stayed with me through all these ups and downs. My sister says she has "true grit."

On the way home, I think some more about this church at Carver Park. I think of the goals I have for the people there. I think of the committed core of that church, and I pray for their growth. They are beginning to see that the gospel must be a "carryout" gospel, something which spills over into the lives of others. I'm glad that some of the people have stopped holding back from God and have gone to work. Some of them help me in so many ways. They are learning to call on the sick and shut-in and to show real concern.

They're beginning to see that salvation and education go hand-in-hand, too. You can't really serve the Lord very well unless you have some good tools, I tell them. We've started a tutorial class on Tuesday and Thursday evenings to help the children with their homework. I shiver when I think how few families turned out at first to receive this help, but the idea is catching on.

It's so easy to be satisfied to stay the way you are. We all have to fight our self-satisfaction continually. If our children can do better in school while they're young, they'll be better servants for Christ in the years ahead. I'm sure of that. I pray for my sons to learn everything they can and to commit their lives to Christ early in life.

As our car eases into the driveway, my boys jump out of the car to set up my wheelchair. My wife opens the car door and helps me pivot from the seat to the chair. I feel so dependent on my family all the time, but I'm thankful they know just what to do.

Inside, we face even more shifting, moving, and managing as they get me settled for late supper and an evening of rest. I realize I may not sleep much tonight. I am still thinking about the service. My mind tends to stay so active that sleep barely comes sometimes. So I just pray and thank God for all He's done. Concentrating on worship causes me to lose sight of everything else—pain, worry, disappointment that comes when I know someone is falling short of the gospel.

When it's late at our house and we still have so much to do, sometimes I'm in danger of letting my temper rise. God hasn't made me perfect, and I have to remind myself and others that He still has a lot of work to do in all of us. But I never try to make excuses for my failures. I don't accept my failures, either. God wants still more of me. I pray and wait on Him for even more of what He has for me. After

No Excuses: God Is More than Sufficient

He's done so much to keep and sustain me, how can I do anything else?

I think of the full day the Lord has given us in church. I am tired from all the activity. But if I had a choice between pushing myself or resting and being more comfortable, I know what I would always choose—to be wearing out for God and holding back nothing from Him. That is the only life worth living.

"Thank You, Lord," I pray, as the lights go out. "I want to wear out serving You."

3
You're Never Too Ill for God

"I've been ill more than I've been well. I don't recall a day without pain since I was fourteen. It hurt one day to play ball, and my father took me to the doctor. From that day to this, I've learned that God can help you through any circumstances."

Dr. Scott Lea was listening to me closely. I was trying to explain how I became as he saw me now. But I wanted him to know there was more than just what he saw. I wanted him to know how God's work in my life has sustained me beyond all expectations.

"I forget about all this pain when I'm serving God," I said. That's what my condition has taught me—how much God can do with me in spite of everything."

Everything—as this doctor sitting with me in his office well knew even better than I—was a form of arthritis so serious it had fused every joint in my body. Mine is one of the worst forms of arthritis: psoriatic arthritis.

"There's just nothing left for the arthritis to attack anymore," Dr. Lea said.

He was gently trying to confirm what I already knew.

I know it's not easy for a doctor to look a patient in the eye and talk about painful things. But it was an understanding we both needed, if we were to work together for my benefit. I had been sent to him at the lowest point in my long history so far. I needed heart surgery. He knew the best heart surgeons in Houston—the famous "DeBakey boys," as he called them. And because I was such a "surgical risk," Dr. Lea took me under his care to arrange the surgery with Dr. Jimmy Howell—the best.

Dr. Lea had discovered I had a heart infection in addition to my severe arthritis with all its other complications. He didn't tell me at the time that most people die from this infection called candida endocarditis. It's an infection growing on the heart valve that can fall off into the bloodstream at any time and spread to the whole body—my certain end.

"I've accepted my arthritis," I said to Dr. Lea, "and all the pain and disability that goes with it. As long as I can function somehow and God can still use me, I don't mind being the way I am. I've stopped bothering God about it. I just need to get through this surgery now. But these fevers—they've kept me down in bed so that I can't serve my people anymore. I've got to get back into my ministry."

I could see from the concern on his face that he wanted to help me. He nodded as I talked. I was sitting in a wheelchair, feeling very weak. I felt the fever breaking out and drying the loose scales of psoriasis that for so long had covered every inch of my skin with lesions. The fever always made my skin pull and itch while the pain pierced my joints from the inside.

"That fever began in late spring," I said. "I'd hardly had a chance to recover from my last medical problem before it started. I just can't seem to get free of the complications from this arthritis. I keep waiting for the end of it all."

The doctor nodded sympathetically. He was a good listener. "It's been one thing after another, hasn't it?" he asked.

"Yes," I answered. "You say that so matter-of-factly, as if you expected to hear me say it. Are you not very surprised that I've been in the hospital more than forty times for one problem after another?"

"No," Dr. Lea said. "I could almost tell you what the problems have been. But you tell me instead."

He paused, and then he said, "All these things which are happening to you are related to the form of arthritis which you have. They come either from the disease itself and the deterioration it has caused or from the intensive medication you've had to take to make the condition bearable."

I felt comfortable with this young doctor. Nothing I could tell him would surprise or excite him. He'd counseled closely with my lifelong physician, Dr. C. C. Smith, and he had asked me to tell him my medical history in my own words, to give him a clearer picture.

When I tell this story to some people, they look skeptical. *Nobody could have all that happen to them!* I can see them thinking. I can see it in their eyes. They don't know how God can sustain you.

This doctor who listened to what I told him was the kind of doctor who would help me by his wisdom. He would add all those facts together and come up with an explanation. He had confirmed my heart infection, based on tests, other evidence, and the suspicions of several doctors who had examined me.

I liked the doctor's openness and his unalarming attitude. He put me at ease.

More than anything, as I told my story, I wanted the doctor to know how I had gotten through all these things. He sat before me well and whole, all that I was not. But I felt a strength welling up within me that did not match my physical condition. I wanted him to understand that strength. I wanted to express the way God Himself, through the power of His Spirit, had so greatly sustained me. "I can do all things through Christ" who strengthens me. That promise from the Bible had carried me so very far.

"The fevers began in the spring of 1983," I said, "just as I'd regained strength following a bad break in my right hip. The break had kept me in bed for several months. I'd broken the artificial socket getting out of my car to pick up some medicine. I remember it was a hot September day because I lay there on the pavement in the sun a long time before somebody came by and discovered me. I was getting along on crutches before then, and I felt I could go anywhere. But when I slipped, the fall dislodged the artificial ball and socket in my hip which had given me good mobility after hip-replacement surgery. I've never been able to get around as well since then.

"The doctors didn't want to operate because of my skin lesions from the chronic psoriasis that goes with my condition. They didn't want to open up my skin and run the risk of infection. So they just put me to bed in traction and let me heal slowly."

Oh, so slowly. Two months in the hospital, and then weeks in bed at home, unable to do a thing but lie there and be waited on—how long it had been. It's the helplessness that is harder than anything else. I can handle the worst kind of pain as long as I can move.

"God has taught me a lot about patience, and He hasn't stopped teaching me yet," I told the doctor. "It's a good thing because today I'm so weak I can't even think of moving around anywhere."

The doctor nodded again, listening hard. "It's the infection," he said. "You'll regain strength soon when we get the fever stopped. We've got to get you to Houston for heart surgery right away."

Heart surgery: that was the last thing in this world I wanted to face. That meant splitting open my chest from top to bottom, breaking my sternum—splitting my rib cage in two, the doctor explained—and removing a valve from my heart, then giving me an artificial valve instead. *I could die,* I thought. I wasn't ready to do that. God had given me too much yet to do. At age forty-one, I had too much left I wanted to do for Him.

Besides, splitting this skin was a major risk in itself. What if the skin refused to heal? What if the incision introduced an infection into my body?

So many layers of my skin had shed since this psoriasis came on me in my twenties when the arthritis first attacked me in earnest. The swollen joints and the arthritis came together in a "package," the doctors said. I had shed enough skin in my life to keep my body cells working double shift around the clock just to keep up with the replacement task of making new skin. No, my skin was nothing to be cutting open for heart surgery.

I would ask my church to pray with me before I went under the surgeon's knife—no matter how famous he was.

"It's such a risk," I said aloud. "I don't know if I'm ready for it."

"You have to be," Dr. Lea said. He looked me straight in the eye. "You have no choice." I knew then that God would have to sustain me. And He would.

What the doctor didn't tell me until months after the surgery—when it became apparent I would indeed survive—was that very few patients—let alone patients with my history—live through the infection I had on my heart. One doctor told Dr. Lea he'd never known of a patient to live through candida endocarditis. Dr. Lea himself would later pronounce it "amazing" that I had survived. But today he was simply trying to urge me toward the surgery quickly.

"You have a very severe yeast infection on the heart

valve," he said. "I've rarely seen one so large. We must remove it at once. We can't wait."

I had no recourse but to trust him and to pray. As I would later learn, it could only have been the prayer and the extended fasting of my congregation, family, and friends that carried me through. I did not know at the time how closely I was facing death. But I did know the power of God to see me through.

"Tell me the rest of your health history," Dr. Lea urged me. "Start at the beginning and move forward. If we keep going backwards, it's harder to follow."

It's funny how the memory runs backward, I thought. That's how I want to tell it—yesterday, and then the day before that. But I would try to start at the beginning.

"My father had arthritis," I said. "His neck was fused, so he couldn't turn his head. And in later years he had trouble getting around. He couldn't whip us boys when we were young, so he'd make us get switches from the trees and whip each other when we were bad! When we were older, we'd have to ride in the car while he drove and turn our heads to tell him if anything was coming because he couldn't turn his head to either side of him. His two brothers had it—one had the bad arthritis and the other had the psoriasis. I must have inherited it all, but I didn't think much about it when I was growing up.

"Then one day I had this nagging pain in my hip. I complained so much my father took me to a doctor who said I had rheumatoid arthritis. Today I know that's about the age the disease first shows up. The doctor decided to remove my tonsils to improve my general health. I remember my first trip to Providence Hospital in Waco. At that time, if you were black, you were put on the bottom floor of the hospital, no matter what your condition. I remember seeing patients in the hallways with curtains around them, it was so crowded. I think that was the first time I became aware of those differences.

"After that surgery, I went on back to school, but I never played sports. I kept score, things like that. But otherwise, my condition didn't make me dysfunctional for several years.

"Then at about age twenty, I really went down with arthritis. There are people who say stress brings it on. I'd had plenty of that. I was married during my senior year of high school, then divorced. That disappointment led me to 'sow some wild oats,' and I abused my health staying up all night, playing cards, and gambling. I'd been raised in a Christian home, but I was ignoring all the things I knew to be right just then. I was going through Paul Quinn College at the time, too. My life was full of pressures.

"One night I was sitting in a restaurant with a date, and she asked me to let her get up from the table for a minute. I suddenly realized I couldn't stand up. My left ankle was swelling up and I had to be taken home. At home we soaked it, and the next day I tried to go to work at a nursery where I'd been doing heavy outdoor work, but I suddenly realized I was unable to function at all. That was the last week I remember having reasonably good health in all my life. I became bedridden for two years.

"Early twenties," Dr. Lea reflected. "That's about the age for the onset of psoriatic arthritis. You seem to have followed the classic pattern."

"Yes, it's been more than twenty years now," I said, and I recalled all the days since then that God had sustained me.

For a while I was very bitter toward God. I had no feeling of commitment to Christ or any sense of salvation. At Paul Quinn College I was learning about Neanderthal man, and this raised a lot of skeptical questions in my mind about creation and the Book of Genesis—things that deeply distressed my father, a devout minister of the gospel. I wondered if God had really created me, and if so, if He had abandoned me.

That same year, 1962, I was in the hospital for fifty-two days and my skin shed like a snake skin. I never realized the human body had that much skin to waste. The shedding had a deep psychological effect on me. The psoriasis had even gotten on my face. It was dry, without pain, and I could just pull it off.

Later that year I was sent to the Warm Springs Hospital for Rehabilitation in Gonzales, Texas. I always felt good about that place. A woman, Dr. Kirkpatrick, got around very well in a motorized wheelchair, so I saw it was possible to get along well even with a handicap. At Gonzales, I also learned to be charming and grateful, all those things which succeeded in getting me the care I needed. I remember rooming with the two other black children at the home—the Bell boys. I learned they later died of multiple sclerosis. I spent a lot of time near dying people in my early twenties.

When I came home three months later I had no improvement, but I'd developed a more open mind about my condition. Early the next year I was sent to John Sealy Hospital in Galveston, Texas, for more diagnostic study. I was put on a large segregated black ward, with dying people all around me. I remember we were all like a brotherhood of survivors in that place. I listened to doctors talking and tried to diagnose things. I learned the problem of a "little knowledge being a dangerous thing," and my fears increased. One day a man died after what I heard the nurses call "unnecessary surgery." I felt I had been the victim of a lot of blood taking because it was a teaching hospital and I felt "used" for the education of these young interns.

It was a degrading experience, and the appearance of my

psoriasis meant even the nurses would shun me. I remember one nurse who would only touch me with a sheet or with gloves on. I've overcome that reaction today, but I was young then and it wasn't easy for me. Now I just offer my arm to someone, rather than my hand, and I make their reaction the "other person's problem," instead of something I have to deal with.

I felt desperate then and I called for my family to come and take me home to die. When I returned home I was on a very high dose of cortisone for my arthritis. My face was moon-shaped from the reaction to the drugs. I knew the cortisone would cause my bones to decalcify and become brittle, so I quit 'cold turkey.' I went from fifty milligrams of a certain type of cortisone to nothing at all overnight. I weighed only seventy-nine pounds and for eight days I ate or drank nothing and vomited a lot. I felt I was at my end.

In desperation, my father took me to a quack doctor in Palestine, Texas. He was a little black man in an apron and a train engineer's cap. He had salt, pepper, and mustard containers, and washed-out whiskey bottles, all filled with medicine. I felt our visit there was an example of the lengths people go to when they are not trusting God to help them.

The next month my father agreed with me and took me to a chiropractor who popped my neck and back—a new sensation—and gave me much relief. He also put me on apple cider, vinegar, and honey. I took no aspirin, antacids, or any other medicine. Gradually, I went from the wheelchair to crutches to being able to walk again. I viewed it as a kind of miracle. I was finally able to return to Paul Quinn College, then I transferred to Baylor University in the summer of 1965. I felt God with me, beginning to lift me up. I began to realize that God had been with me all along, even when I was not aware of it.

I attended Baylor University for the summer and fall of 1965, then had a relapse in January of 1966 and was back up again in May. I'd not been admitted to law school due to low grades on the admission test—a great disappointment to me. However, I felt the Lord calling me to preach, and I remembered I'd said to Him, "Lord, if You get me up this time, I believe I'll do what You want me to do." Very soon, during a church service, I accepted my calling to preach.

I finished at Baylor with a degree in education and was placed for student teaching and later for employment in an all-white junior high in Waco. This situation could have caused added stress, but I discovered that the myth I'd been told—whites are smarter than blacks—wasn't true. I taught ninth-grade history and enjoyed the classes very much. I went through three years with very little psoriasis and developed a high tolerance for the pain that was constantly with me. Over the years I've learned to be in severe pain and still function.

I paused in my story and looked at Dr. Lea. He was still listening intently. I knew I'd told him a lot that was not strictly medical, but somehow it gave background for what was happening to me physically. It also gave Dr. Lea some idea of the balance at first between my good health and my down spells. I'm always thankful for that three-year period in my twenties when I was up and functioning well. Near the end of that time, my father died in 1968. And in 1969 I married my wife, Elwayne. Her parents were upset about that prospect and tried to prevent the marriage, but she has stayed with me faithfully. Her parents knew what she maybe only vaguely guessed—how much care I would need as time went on. Dr. Lea had commented during one of her sessions on her faithfulness to me. Her support and the support of my church were the elements that carried me through the very worst health crises, he said. God has surely blessed me to have provided that support.

Shortly after our marriage I had another health setback and was down for several months, then up again. I had been in graduate school at Baylor and was assistant director of the Upward Bound program. Those stresses may have aggravated my health, so I quit graduate school. I've spent my life taking on stressful situations. Sometimes I think I thrive on them. But I have to learn how much stress is enough—how much God wants me to take on.

I began going to a black doctor in Calvert who was eighty years old. He seemed able to help me as no one else had done. He had graduated from Meharry Medical College in Nashville, Tennessee. Due to prejudice against black doctors, even in 1970, he felt he had to dispense his own drugs rather than trust the local pharmacy, he told me. So he would prepare his own pills and put them in little bottles with labels which read, "Take one red pill and two blue pills." This doctor kept me going for two years until he became sick. I really give him a lot of credit for helping me.

In spring of 1970 I had a bad setback and went into Hillcrest Baptist Hospital in Waco. I felt I might die, and I had sensations of being "sometimes here, and sometimes there" in a floating feeling. I was sent to the Methodist hospital in Houston where I was given a new wonder drug. I was told it could affect my immune system, so I prayed with some friends, including Dr. Dan McGee of Baylor University. We knew my decision was a risk, but it was one I was willing to take. At the time I was not working, except to serve the two small country churches where my father had preached, one in Bremond and one in Chilton, Texas. Through the preaching, I began to understand what God could do with my life. I began to sense a larger calling.

"The new drug seemed to have a wonderful effect. It put me in remission for five years, from age thirty to thirty-five. I held several positions including an economic-advancement position to find jobs for minorities. I became very active in political affairs in Waco, and for a while there was hardly an affirmative-action decision made where I was not somehow involved. I also served on the school board during that time and was responsible for several affirmative-action decisions in the school system. Those were stressful times, but I felt useful and good about what I was doing.

Then came a major setback after five good years. I began to have dizzy spells and went to Scott and White Memorial Hospital in Temple, Texas. My physician was called out of the country shortly after I arrived, and his assistant decided the new "wonder" drug was starting to affect my body negatively so he took me off the medicine. When my own specialist returned and discovered what had happened, he tried to reintroduce me to the medication, but my body would no longer respond to it. My life began a downward cycle of health problems which I trace to that reversal.

Dr. Lea was looking troubled by my story now, so I paused.

"You know," he said, "The new drug causes several problems. Some of the things you're probably about to tell me may have resulted from that drug. I wouldn't be too hard on the doctor who made that decision."

I heard his plea. I knew I'd have to leave it to God to understand why these things happen as they do. Ultimately, my life is in His hands. The important thing was that He was still at work in my life, more powerfully today than ever.

I do know that I took seriously the call of God in my life to full-time service just about when that setback happened —within a year. Maybe my increased dependency upon Him led me to see that I had to trust Him with everything.

My present church in Carver Park called me to serve and I accepted. I said to the people, 'You know my health history,' and they welcomed me anyhow. They are an unusual church, and their faith has been tested, as has mine, by my illnesses. I began serving there in April, 1978, at age thirty-six. I have been there ever since, and God has blessed me as never before, even as my health has encountered the most serious testings of my life. I wish I had entered full-time Christian service sooner.

In March of 1980, I went to Houston to have an artificial hip implanted. I thought this would give me greater mobility. It was elective surgery, and I felt at peace about it. This was my second hip replacement. I'd had the first one in 1975. But while I was recovering in the hospital, something terrible began to happen to me. My bladder swelled like a balloon due to a fistula or hole in it which led to my colon, so the two organs were "communicating" with each other. Suddenly, I needed colon surgery in a "live-or-die" situation.

I asked to be sent home to pray with my congregation. Prayer with them was all I needed to come back in peace on Monday. The doctors operated on my abdomen, removing part of my colon and closing the hole in my bladder. All this was a terrible trauma to my body. But I went through the ordeal in faith and took my testimony home to the church. The more they saw God testing me, the more they seemed to come to me with their own trials.

A year later, my arthritis again began to cause so much pain I went to a hospital in Austin—to no avail. Their remedy was antidepressants, so they sent me home with some. The antidepressants affected my spirits and my body terribly, and I said to myself, *Here you are, a man of God, depending on drugs for peace of mind.* So I gave up the medicine, believing

God Himself would lift me up. I found a local doctor named Herman White who taught me to use the powers of the mind to concentrate on good health.

About a year later in spring, 1982, I returned to the hospital for unexplained episodes of fever. I felt it was one thing after another now, and I wondered how much faith God was requiring of me. The doctors discovered that I had a bowel obstruction, a complication from my former surgery which I've learned was related also to my arthritic condition. More surgery was called for. I weighed only eighty-six pounds and still felt very low. The doctors force-fed me through my veins to raise my weight to 112 pounds and readied me for surgery. I remember the anesthesiologist asking me to turn my head to the right or the left. My neck was fused from my arthritis so I couldn't turn it, and there was some question of how I would be safely put to sleep. When I finally awoke from the surgery, I remember saying to my wife, "Thank God, I'm alive!" I knew as never before that God had what it takes for every situation. I returned home in June of 1982, ever confident in God.

In July, 1982—I never shall forget it—I was in church for the first time since my surgery. Everybody was clapping and praising the Lord. The chairman of the deacons stood and made a speech, and then he passed out. At the end of the service I was placed in my car; then I learned that my deacon had died. My first thought was to go and minister to his wife, so I went to see her. She asked me to preach the funeral sermon. I had so recently looked death in the face myself, so I decided to give a sermon on the "intensive care" of God. I was trembling and had to sit in a chair to give the message, as I always have to do now. Then, as now, no matter how I feel, someone else needs me and wants my help. I find healing for myself in serving others.

You're Never Too Ill for God

By September, I felt good enough to be moving around, preaching regularly, giving the Lord everything I had. Even though the arthritis in my body had claimed every joint, making me increasingly helpless, that never stopped me. As long as I was working for the Lord, I knew I could overcome pain and every other obstacle.

Then, without warning, I was down again. I fell getting out of the car—I could still drive then—and dislodged my hip. I found myself down in bed again for recovery, and during that time I developed a fever which my body could not overcome.

Dr. Lea was still listening. He smiled. I would add one more thing to my story. I said, "Through it all, my only desire has been to give God public credit for everything He's done for me. When I'm down with some sickness, I simply come back ready to do more for Him than ever before. I develop an increasing vision for my ministry."

"You're doing exactly the right thing to follow that desire," Dr. Lea said. "That driving vision is what has kept you going all these years. You've suffered more problems and surgeries than most people have ever been through in a lifetime. So many of us would have given up, or we'd have died long ago from the surgical trauma. I mean that. Without the kind of faith you're talking about, most people can't handle what you've been through. But here you are, facing this next ordeal of heart surgery with all the faith and support of your church, your family, and your inner strength. You have resources that few people have. I believe you'll be all right."

I thanked God for the doctor's words. I felt he understood what God had done for me so far. I knew how many people would be praying, even when I felt so ill I was unable to pray. I knew that God would lift me up and keep me going as I faced heart surgery.

My heart surgery did indeed bring me to the ultimate test of God's care for me. Today, on the other side of that ordeal, I am still weak when I would like to run or to walk. But I know from firsthand experience the strength God can provide in the most desperate of circumstances.

I'm alive, and even the doctors are surprised. I'm serving God, and my people are still calling on me to help them. More than ever before I've known firsthand the power of God to lift me up and keep me going on for Him.

4
Depression: God Can Heal Our Minds

We can be victorious in life. We can overcome the biggest threat of all—the threat of depression. Depression robs us of hope. It prevents us from believing in God's plan for our lives.

I've learned that depression is temporary. It feels permanent every time it comes. But God finds ways to get us through the hardest of times. It's most often prayer—ours and the prayer of others who support us when we can't help ourselves—that breaks the bonds of the darkest hours.

I think depression comes most easily when we're afraid God has abandoned us, and our lives have no purpose or meaning. We feel the heavy weight of unending hopelessness. We fear we are unable to be what God intends.

I think this depression is far worse than any physical problem I've ever had. When I lack strength, I sometimes think God lacks it, too. I forget that He never changes, no matter how my body and my mind are pained and distressed. At those times, I've learned again and again how God can meet us in our darkest hours.

I've learned that believing prayer—above all else—is the way out. I've learned to be grateful for the prayers of others. I believe Christians can help one another in these dark times more than they ever imagine.

We need to pray for one another. I thank God for praying friends. And I thank Him most of all that He is the kind of God who delivers us with unexplainable power and grace.

My worst depression set in after my heart surgery. I had been through such an ordeal that the healing which followed should have been an upward path. But it wasn't. I felt myself sinking lower and lower, as if God were through with my life.

I know today how much prayer was going up for me through all that time. People at my church were praying. During the surgery they fasted and prayed around the clock for me. They continued until I was declared out of danger. And then they sustained me in prayer for many months afterwards.

My sister reported that the fasting was difficult for some, but their discomfort helped them feel closer to me in prayer. I'm sure that's true because some unusual power seemed to carry me through the physical crisis of surgery. Praying friends somehow provided that extra cooperation with God. Even the best heart surgeon in the world can only do so much without the quickening power of God to supply a healing response.

I felt a great sense of triumph as God did the impossible. He had seen me through very dangerous surgery. For weeks after that my wife, my deacons, and my friends cared for me and transported me to the hospital for daily medication. I felt the upward pull of recovery in my body.

Then something happened within my mind to delay my progress. Today the doctor says a sudden mental setback produced a physical one. Indeed, many of our setbacks begin in the mind.

I began to run a fever the very day a friend of mine died. I felt the ghost of death haunting me. My lifelong friend, John Westbrook, had received his call to the ministry very

Depression: God Can Heal Our Minds 51

close to the same time I did. We had served in a lot of churches together. We had both vowed an all-out commitment to Christ. Now he was gone, after a successful ministry to the largest black church in downtown Houston, Antioch Baptist Church—a church which was founded by freed slaves in the 1860s. My friend was dead, suddenly and unexpectedly, and here I was, struggling to be God's person in an upward battle with pain. I felt I should have been taken and he left. As these thoughts circled, depression sank over me.

Then, within days, another very young man who received his call to preach in my church, Bobby Bradshaw, also died unexpectedly. I wondered again why I had been left behind.

My fever burned and my energy sank lower. I felt abandoned by God. I had to return to the hospital, and Dr. Lea began looking for the cause of my relapse and continuing fever. Today he says my reaction to those deaths was the main cause of my flaring fever. At that time, he began looking closely for further infection in my body—either in the wires that bound my sternum following the chest surgery or from the catheter inserted to give me daily medication. He removed the catheter and we waited to see if the fever would subside. I lay in bed, first in the hospital and then at home, too ill even to think or pray for myself. I could do nothing but wait.

It's strange how, even on those days, God steps in to show us there is something we can still do. I was feeling so ill, and a friend came by to discuss her own search for God's will in her life. I could see her looking at me as if I had the answers she needed. That's how people keep responding to me, as if this ordeal has made me fit to offer them unusual strength. God somehow seems to give me the words to help, even when I am at lowest ebb.

As we talked, a knock came at the door. A man who was

chopping down a tree in my backyard came in for payment. He entered the room where we were talking and said, "My, you are a pretty lady," to my visitor, as if he intended to stay for a while. I wondered at his interruption, but I began to talk with him. Soon he said, "I didn't know you are a minister."

"Yes," I said. "That's why I wanted you to chop the wood today, instead of on Sunday."

"Well, it's a hard life out there," the man said. "I have to work when I can get it."

"If you give one day to the Lord, He'll take care of you," I urged him.

"I go to church with my sister on Sunday night," he said. "And sometimes with a neighbor on Saturday."

"Oh, then you're all right," I said, looking closely at him. "I'll call you if I have any other work."

"Thanks," the man said. "And I want you to know, I'll come back. I don't care if you're blue or pink or what color you are. I'll come back."

I thought that was an odd statement, but I saw him glancing at my friend, who was also white. I realized he was trying to be a part of whatever was going on in our conversation. I felt, too, that he was trying to tell me that he had some needs which he hoped someone—only God, of course—could supply.

"God bless you," I said. He broke into an uneven smile.

When he left, I suddenly realized I felt feverish and dry. But during the time he had talked with us, I hadn't thought for a minute about how I was feeling. God uses others to take our minds off ourselves.

We are never left alone to survive impossible bouts with depression. God is always there. He knows what we need. So many people have shown me that. My lifetime friend,

Depression: God Can Heal Our Minds

Allen Kuykendall, came to my bedside one day and prayed with me. Though we had been friends for as many years as we could remember, we had never prayed together. He said he had been feeling a call to the ministry, and I could see it in his changed approach to our friendship and his eagerness to pray with me. God often works through friends, putting our needs on their hearts at just the right time.

Close to that time, others who were concerned for me began to feel a need to pray for my recovery. I lay at home, knowing they had gathered to pray. My fever had inched downward that day, even as they began. Then the next day, after they had prayed, it raged again.

"It doesn't matter," one of these faithful friends declared. "God has heard us." Sure enough, the next day the fever went down again and returned to nearly normal. The doctor canceled tests he had planned for me.

Those who knew me and participated in that prayer time felt God's touch as much as I. It's something we can never explain except to give thanks and worship when we feel God's touch. It gives us a respect for prayer. It makes us want to pray all the more.

I've passed through many dark days with no promise that my body will ever be free of pain. But God seems to hold His hand over me each time I face a new ordeal, to lift up my mind and my spirit. What a different experience this is from taking medicine for depression. Medicine leaves me feeling weak. God empowers me.

Once during a spell of physical weakness that put me in the hospital for a few days, a doctor recommended I take a drug for depression because I was having trouble coming out of my discouragement. I decided to try his advice, and I took the drug for about a week. By the end of the week, my body felt so relaxed and lifeless that my despair increased. I felt

I would never be able to move or do anything for myself again. I decided that the medicine was giving me a false sense of helplessness through its power to relax me. I needed to feel I was getting hold of my life, not losing my hold on it even more. So again I stopped taking the medicine. I decided that whatever physical or mental problem I was fighting, the drug was worse than the original problem.

My problem this time had certainly been a serious one, triggering my depression. I was feeling restless because I was so dependent now on other people to take care of all my needs. I wished the doctors could recommend something that would give me a higher level of health. Instead, I was hospitalized again, unexpectedly. I had suffered another sudden loss of memory for about two hours, just as I'd finished preaching at a special evening service. Anyone who knows me would have said it was because I overdid myself that day—I was in my church all morning for special services, traveled to a country church to preach at 3 PM, then turned around and hurried back to Waco to preach at a 7:30 PM service. I knew I was very tired and should rest, but my schedule only allowed about thirty minutes rest all day. I've had to learn to pace myself better, but this day I had overestimated what my body could do. That's a lesson everyone keeps telling me to work on—to save my energy, so I can do my best every time I'm needed. "Don't make so many promises to people," they tell me.

At any rate, I was in for a surprise that would again send me into depression. When I checked into the hospital, I was very worried. I'd always felt I could keep going, as long as my mind was clear. That's the one thing I've felt I absolutely must have in order to do God's work.

After their examinations, the doctors came to me and tried to prepare me for the worst news possible. The tests they had given me showed that I might have a problem on my

Depression: God Can Heal Our Minds

brain—an abscess or a lesion, they said. Brain surgery might be necessary, they said. "Don't be afraid to cry if you need to," they said, and then they left me alone to work through their tough and difficult news. I prayed—knowing God was there.

I lay in bed all day wondering how God would help me through this ordeal. I decided I would accept no more surgery. I felt I had endured all I could, and I felt my thinking processes were too vital to allow the risk of brain surgery. I just couldn't take that risk.

I don't know when I have ever felt so low.

I wondered what God could do. Some of my friends began to pray again, and I learned once more what the prayers of others can do for me. I learned again about the grace of God in my life.

Friends assured me that God would intervene—that God loved me and cared for me more than I was presently able to understand. "No, this cannot be!" a friend had said in prayer to God, and felt God agreeing. God was confirming that I must continue my ministry. It was His work and He would hold me up.

I soon began to feel the power of that prayer. I felt myself gaining some expectancy to see what God would do. I had many visitors, even as I lay there in my distress. My visitors all wanted me to counsel them and to reassure *them* of God's goodness. Somehow I found myself saying to them the very words I needed to hear. "Pray, and let God work," I said.

Those words were God's words for me. The peace of God was what I needed most—more than anything physical. I prayed for my fears to be relieved and my trust to increase. God wanted to strengthen my faith, and He again gave me the assurance that when I have faith, He has power.

The next day the doctors came back to me.

"We have changed our minds," they said. "Our second test showed nothing at all. This second test was a more sophisticated test. All it showed us was an old scar, not a lesion or an abscess. We think this scar was left from your memory loss right before your heart surgery. There's no other indication of any problem."

No problem? I thought. *An old scar? Nothing more at all?* I was at a loss for words. They saw me struggling to find the right words to thank them. I wanted to thank God so they would know what a victory I felt. I told everyone who came to see me that God answers prayer.

"Your brain is in excellent condition," the doctors said. "You have nothing to worry about."

Nothing to worry about: How worried I had been! I wondered if the doctors believed in miracles. I kenw some of them did, in their deepest thoughts. I knew most would say it was just the scientific results of a "sophisticated test" that helped them discover I had no problems. But they had certainly seemed worried just the day before. Whatever their explanations, I knew that God had worked one more saving grace in my life. He had brought me to the brink of death, only to show me His grace.

I certainly believe God gave us doctors to help us. I can testify to how much they've been able to do for me. But beyond medical help, I continue to say to God, "Here is my condition. I'm waiting on You for what to do." And God has never failed to lift me up.

In fact, it is usually at my lowest point, as I give up, that God does His will. I know I need to come to that point of trust sooner. When I have a problem, I need to understand how much God wants to do for me. I need always to seek His grace and His Spirit.

I know as well as anyone that when you're depressed, it

Depression: God Can Heal Our Minds

is the hardest time of all to seek the Lord. Anyone who has ever had physical or mental illness knows that. You tend to feel abandoned. You feel so low you don't have the energy to lift yourself up even enough to pray. In fact, you feel like you have a physical problem. But that is what we must do.

I think the feeling of depression is the closest thing to experiencing death. I want to stop eating, to stop talking to people, to stop doing anything to help myself. My emotions and inner feelings seem to die. I don't want to live. My life seems to stop and wither away. I know these feelings are mental and have nothing to do with the physical facts of my survival. My mind has somehow shut down. My life stops.

Once when I was feeling low I read the book about Joni Eareckson Tada and how she overcame the depression of her crippling accident. I gained so much inspiration from reading her testimony. She still had hope, in spite of everything. I decided that hers is the attitude God intends for us to have—we must hope in spite of everything.

There's a secret to having that hope, I'm finding. We absolutely have to look beyond our present circumstances and focus upon God and His love.

We need the fellowship of other Christians. We need the love and prayer support of others more than we need any other thing in this world. God has very graciously reminded us in the Bible not to forsake the "assembling of ourselves together" (Heb. 10:25). We were never meant to walk this life alone.

My doctors tell me that I do as well as I do because I have so much "support." That is the word they use: *support* from family, friends, and a praying church.

My most blessed experience of support has been a prayer band which meets every Tuesday in a different home. The members of this band of fellow Christians decided one day that I needed special prayer. They came to me with the idea of meeting to pray for me. They could see that the recent ordeal over the brain surgery had left me feeling very low for several days. Somehow I couldn't shake the aftereffects of that frightening experience. I wanted so much to get moving again, and I felt so tired. I began to worry about the burden I was to my family. That thought made me even more tired. These worries were all things over which I felt I had no control. The thought of having no control made me feel even weaker yet.

My friends knew they must help me break the cycle of despair over helplessness. They believed that our prayers together would increase the power of God to lift me up. How right they were!

As we met each Tuesday night, I began to feel the power of believing faith in a new way. I found the Lord speaking to me about anger and frustration, attitudes that were holding me back from getting hold of myself. I thought of the verse, "Let not the sun go down upon your wrath" (Eph. 5:26*b*), and I realized that many frustrations connected with my immobility were weighing on me. I was feeling angry with the people who were supposed to be helping me the most. Perhaps I was angry at God because of my condition. Somehow through the prayer I began to let go of that anger each evening. I've been able to go to sleep with a clear mind, holding no thoughts that would disturb me through the night.

Even in a normal situation many things upset us. People never seem to do what we think they should. They delay our plans, keep us waiting, and dash cold water on our best dreams. In a time of weakness, their frustrations seem even more difficult to handle. So the danger of harboring anger becomes even more keen. Through prayer and leaning on the prayer support of others, I've found I can overcome the

Depression: God Can Heal Our Minds

anger which builds my depression. Now when I go to sleep I have to let everything go and let God take it. The problems that distress me are not solved. But the bitterness within my heart is gone.

Because I have been gripped by depression, I know how to help others who have felt this agony. I've had people drive to my house and sit by my bedside to hear what I have to say to them. I marvel that they would want to sit beside me in my weakness and ask me to point them out of depression. They have such confidence that I know the way back to wholeness. I pray that God will sustain me to give them the answers they need.

I've found there is always a therapy in helping others. Being open to give of yourself is one of my best medicines for my own sense of helplessness. God always uses these visitors to give me a renewed sense of purpose and hope. As they listen and receive help from the Lord I realize that no life is ever too cast down for God to use it. In fact, God seems to use me more, the more trouble I experience.

I'm convinced that God always has a way through. I like to point people to 2 Corinthians 4:8-9. Paul said, "We are hard pressed on every side, but not crushed" (NIV). He said we are "perplexed, but not in despair; . . . cast down, but not destroyed." Paul himself knew about depression, and he knew the way through it.

He said depression could even bring good results, if we let God use it. It is a way of dying with Jesus, "That the life also of Jesus might be made manifest in our body" (v. 10). He added, "For we which live are alway delivered unto death for Jesus' sake, that the life also of Jesus might be made manifest in our mortal flesh" (v. 11).

Depression is a form of death, and God offers life in its

place. God is the source of life. No darkness is ever too serious for His intervention.

When we feel deeply depressed we cannot believe that God already knows the way out. That is when we most need to turn to the Scriptures and see what God says about our condition. We must pray the believing prayer that says, "I know you have a way for me."

God has never failed me. God knows the way up from depression, as I place myself firmly in His hands and wait for Him. He has led me out of darkness so many times, I know He can do it for anyone.

Rev. Robert Gilbert and fellow staff members of Upward Bound Program, Baylor University, 1968

Installation ceremony of board members of the Waco Independent School District Board of Trustees, June 1976—seated: Mrs. Howard Hagar, John Faulkner, James Hawkins, standing: Ray Hicks, Phillip McCleary, Dr. Emma L. Harrison, Rev. Robert Gilbert

Pastor Gilbert (right, rear) and the Usher Board of Carver Park Baptist Church in 1978, Sisters R. Smith, president, E. Harris, secretary, L. Calvin, assistant secretary, E. Irvin, treasurer, and Brother B. Irvin, parliamentarian

Pastor Gilbert the same year with the Junior Ushers Unit

Pastor Gilbert and the Deacons of Carver Park (1978).

Brother Gilbert receives a plaque, "A Warrior for Mankind," at the John Adams Center of Paul Quinn College in 1979. The presentation was made by William Toliver (Paul Quinn College Photo).

Brother Gilbert, his wife Elwayne, and their sons Ja Ja and Kenyatta pose in their Sunday best (1979).

The church has honored Brother Gilbert with days of appreciation. In 1979 Rev. Gilbert, his wife, and his mother, Mrs. Fannie Gilbert-Robinson, sat at the head table (Davis Studio Photo).

Paul Quinn College in 1984 announced a scholarship to be given to deserving students in honor of Brother Gilbert (Paul Quinn College Photo)

Brother Gilbert at the entrance of Providence Hospital, Waco, entering for outpatient treatment following heart surgery (1983)

Rev. Gilbert and Rev. Cleo LaRue discuss community issues at Tolliver's Chapel Baptist Church, May 1987.

Celebrating the eightieth birthday of Brother Gilbert's mother, Mrs. Gilbert-Robinson, are his sister, LaRue Dorsey, and brothers Charles E. R. Gilbert, Benotha T. Gilbert, and Rev. Samuel J. Gilbert, January, 1987 (Photo by Lloyd B. Walker, Houston).

5
Poverty: Blessing in Disguise

Some folks would say if you're born poor, you don't have a chance. If they'd seen where I was born, they'd have written me off. But there are blessings in having less. You can dream and believe many things are possible. God always rewards believing faith, we were always told. We knew without question He was taking care of us.

Most of all, we believed God was looking after us from the very beginning and that we were special to Him. Our early struggles give me perspective and compassion today. I don't want to forget where I came from and what God has been able to do with what we began with.

I'm convinced that the condition so many call poverty—not having everything others seem to have—can bring us closer to God. Poverty in itself is surely not a good thing. But some of the values our family and others developed as we lived together in the same neighborhood with little of this world's goods strengthened us for later life. I believe God richly blesses us in any condition when we are truly His children.

My home—2725 South Ninth Street—was a small house that leaned slightly to one side. In cold weather we stuffed rags in the cracks of the windows and covered them with cardboard to keep out the cold. Our house did not look like the birthplace of anyone special by some people's standards. But then, what does anyone know about such things? God was at work among us.

If I came out of what some people call "needy circumstances," so did we all in that neighborhood everyone called "Butcher Pen." Most people in Waco had electricity and indoor plumbing in their homes. We had outdoor toilets and kerosene lamps, like everyone I grew up with. My family had chickens in the yard, which had to be fed every day, and a vegetable garden which gave us some of the best food I've ever eaten. In my mind I can still see that yard and that house.

I came from a praying family. Father was a minister to two country churches and we all knew without doubt what God expected of us. Every Sunday morning we would be at the breakfast table for devotions. We each read a Scripture, and we had prayer around the table. No matter how old we were, we were expected for family devotions if we lived in that house. Today when we encounter problems we remember things our father said to us from the Scriptures about his experience with God. Growing up with Christ foremost in our family is still our richest inheritance.

Father remains in my mind as a special inspiration because he was crippled just as I am. His neck was fused so he couldn't turn his head. He told me a tree fell on him and broke his neck at age twenty-one. But he also seemed to have my kind of arthritis. He couldn't whip us very well because he was so stiff, but he insisted on discipline. So he would have us get switches from the tree and whip each other while he stood and watched. We knew the difference between right and wrong. Father made sure of that.

I don't know what others outside our neighborhood thought of us during those growing-up years. We were always a little community unto ourselves, isolated from the rest of the city except when our parents went to work over in the more prosperous neighborhoods. Unless you had lived where we did, you couldn't know how closely we looked after each other, how tied we were to our church and our school. My best friend Allen Kuykendall and I were really raised by each other's parents. Whatever house we played in, those parents were responsible for us, disciplined us, and gave us what they saw we needed.

Most of all, as children, we learned to dream together. We dreamed of a future different from our everyday world, a day when every one of us would be strong, successful, and good, and nothing would stand in our way.

We dreamed those dreams as we played near the ditch which ran along the front of our houses. In summer the water was low, except when it would fill up with unexpected rain.

That ditch! Ask anyone from Butcher Pen and that ditch will be the scene of their best memories. Over across town, folks were saying it was "too bad about the poor people in South Waco," but we children were dreaming our dreams and laying our plans from our favorite and magical location. On long, hot summer nights we played "marbles for keeps" until twilight, then told each other tall tales, stories of bravery, good fortune, and winning against all odds in the game of life.

Sitting down under the rickety wooden bridge which ran overhead across the ditch, we told our jokes and our stories, and not one of us was poor anymore, nobody was inferior, and the world was turned upside down from the way we understood it to be outside. We were not on the bottom. We always won in every tale we told, and the people on top always lost. We learned to tell these stories from the adults.

We had listened as they sat on the porches and told these same stories to one another, creating their own more sophisticated versions. The stories were a kind of recreation for everyone. More than that, they were a private way of combating what we could not yet change. They made us all feel good somehow.

Somehow this kind of play was as serious as work to all of us because of the ambitions we allowed ourselves to dream of. But sometimes our playing became dangerous. Two friends and I were playing on a piece of heavy earth-moving equipment one time. I touched it and it started up. My two friends, Charles Littlefield and Leo Estelle, jumped off and left me on the machine. It started to move, and I began pulling at the gears and yelling. It reared up and headed toward the houses. Finally, I pulled a gear, it stopped, and my sister, who was ten years older, came out of the house and spanked me. That was the most frightening thing I can ever remember except for the frightening things that happened to my baby brother. He was five years younger and always wanted to follow me around, which I resented. Once he locked himself in a closet by accident, and we thought we'd never get him out. Another time he fell on a milk bottle and cut himself badly. Worst of all, we were playing near the ditch, and he fell off the bannister of the bridge and tumbled into the water. The water was deep that day and I couldn't swim, so we began yelling. My brother B. T., who was home from the military, just happened to come by and rescue him. It's curious how these frightening experiences always stay with you. I'll never forget any of them. They seem to be part of the preparation for life.

The real preparation for life was learning to work hard. We learned the value of hard work early. It's a lesson few children learn today in the same way that so many of us learned it. Boys my age pulled cotton in the fields to help their families. Many of the girls learned to clean, wash, and care for the sick—things their grandmothers taught them as necessary information to make it through this life. I don't know of many young people today who can work as hard as we all learned to work. Father would take us to the cotton fields to help him earn the major source of income for our family. My grandmother, whose house we lived in, came with us too. She was Father's mother and she always went with us, even in her seventies. She and Father would pick the cotton and throw it in the middle of the row for me. Grandmother would gather up the cotton in her apron first. She had made me a little sack, and I'd pick up the cotton for them. That saved them from leaning over to pick it up. As a minister, Father also earned about forty dollars a week at his country church. We earned $1.25 per one-hundred pounds of cotton. All the money any of us earned was pooled within the family. Much of our cotton money was for school clothes. No matter how much I picked as I grew older, it all went to the family, except sometimes I could keep my Saturday earnings. When I got older I could pull 450 to 480 pounds of cotton a day. I weighed only 112 pounds, and I pulled a ninety-pound sack. That may have been hard on my body as I think back today. But I never shied away from working hard.

After the cotton-field days, Dad had contracts to clean windows in new houses being built over near the Veteran's Administration Hospital. It was a cold job, being outside in all that weather, and I didn't like it. We did the work after school and on Saturdays, and earned fourteen dollars per house. Some of the money was used to send my sister to college. Many of those years as we children were older, Mother also worked as a domestic worker in several homes in town including the Blackburns, who were high up in Citizens Bank, and the Pearsons. Everyone worked to contribute to the family. Mother's money went for school clothes for us kids. When she was home, I also remember her working very hard all the time. We kids hauled water from a pipe outside for her to do our laundry and cleaning. Mother made a big fuss about everything always being clean. That's one of my main memories of her.

When I was thirteen, Dad went into the service-station business, and I would wash cars, grease them, and fix flats. We ran the Cities Service Station on the corner of Eighth Street and LaSalle. I remember all the preachers we knew would come and hang out there to talk to my father. But Dad went in the hole because he was too lenient and gave too much credit. He just couldn't make a go of it. By age fourteen, I took caddying jobs at the Municipal Golf Club, and about then I began to take kitchen jobs, first at George's Chef which is called Surf and Sirloin today. I washed dishes, bused tables, cooked rolls, and did all that for three years. I drew my first checks on this job. I worked at other restaurants out in Waco when I was older, including the cafeteria at Baylor, where I was later admitted and became the first black graduate. (At the time I worked there, such a thing had never been considered.) I also worked in restaurants at some distance from home and had to drive clear across town to get there. This was a risky experience for me late at night because of suspicious feelings among white people about black people being in their part of town. I try to forget that now. I try only to think how hard all of us always worked, and what a difference it has made. I think the difference work made was that we all knew we had a goal: to move ahead, become educated, and make something of ourselves.

My parents taught us the value of education. I think we

appreciated education more because we knew the sacrifices everyone made for each other. My parents saw that I got out of the fields when it was time for school. Father intended for us all to receive the best education possible. My sister was the oldest. When she graduated from high school, the rest of us sent her to college at Mary Allen College in Crockett, Texas, and later she went summers to Texas Southern University in Houston for her master's degree in teaching. She was supposed to go to work to send the next child to college. My next brother, B.T., went into the marines instead. But LaRue helped me and my brother Sam when we were in school. Sam is a minister today, as I am, and we never forgot our sister's help to us. I remember that she bought me shoes, and she bought my horn to play in the school band. We always knew we were to help one another. Even today, my sister helps me with whatever she has. That's what families are for.

School was only a few steps from any of our houses—two blocks at the most for almost everyone, and we all had the same teachers. Today we exchange memories about them—which ones would rap us on the knuckles, which ones insisted we get our lessons, and which ones helped us to enjoy learning. Three of my early teachers, Miss Brown, Miss Prather, and Miss Younger, also had taught my father. Oakwood Elementary was a school rich in family heritage.

I have to mention some of these teachers because teachers, ministers, and leaders who were educated became role models for the rest of us. Their presence among us said we could all become something if we tried. There was Miss Prather, stern and tall, quick to rap us on the knuckles to get our attention. There was Mrs. Hamilton, who believed my story when I got a friend in trouble, so that Lorenzo Austin got blamed for something I did. I remember feeling a lot of guilt that I was able to sway things to my side. Mrs. Ewing was tough on us and would use her fist or knuckles on our back if we misbehaved. But in third grade, I got to sing a solo in "Who Stole the Tarts?" a play directed by Mrs. O. W. Jefferson, and I learned the feeling of standing out for doing something special. Miss Cotton did a lot of chastising in fourth grade. In fifth grade, I found the teacher who really helped me set some goals. Miss Younger talked about black history, Adam Clayton Powell, and Charles Drew. She made me want to be a lawyer and go to Washington. Miss Younger owned real estate; she had a very forceful personality and a lot of black pride. She singled me out to do special work for her, and I will never forget what that did for me. Then Mrs. Jefferson encouraged me in the school choir in sixth grade, so my two talents—singing and leading other people—began to emerge through what those teachers did for me. By seventh grade Mrs. Arnold—who always wore red and even had red in the lining of her casket when she died—encouraged me to learn the Gettysburg Address and gave me public-speaking opportunities. I began to get a feel for "who I am."

That other side of who I am also found a model in Mr. R. E. Bevis, our school principal. I realize now, looking back, that he had a skin disease and always looked burned. Everyone remembers him for that. But he did some nice things for me like choosing me to be on the school safety patrol and encouraging me after I won a prize on Washington's birthday for finding the most words in the letters forming Washington's name. This award seemed like a "message" to me somehow that I would achieve even more.

We were aware, also, of adults in our neighborhood who were making something of themselves. Their presence with us was very important. Mr. Manning, who lived in the next block, had a son, Dr. Ruben Manning, who became president of Paul Quinn College and then of Jarvis College. Ruben's sister Lillian was a social worker and another brother, Monroe, was a lieutenant colonel in the military. The Richardsons had two daughters who became teachers, and the Littlefield's son, Harry, became a coach in Beaumont, Texas, and in Los Angeles. Rev. George J. Johnson became the first black to run for the school board in the 1950s. He had a vision about leadership and our people and he was often quoted in the newspaper, which we thought was very significant. We were always told we could do what these older people had done if we were willing to work hard enough to be "twice as good" as anybody else. That's what it would take, we were told.

A lot of our values were learned from grandparents who lived with us and reminded us of the virtues that make for a good person. My grandmother had a lot of wisdom on almost every subject. I respected her ability to cook delicious food from leftovers, including the feet, neck, and every part of a chicken. She never wasted anything. She also baked wonderful biscuits and made special sauces for desserts. To eat at our table was to believe we were rich. Grandmother knew home remedies, too: nine drops of turpentine, a little salt, pepper or sugar in a mixture, and some cooking oil or bacon fat on a white rag if you stepped on a nail. She knew all the secrets of home cures. She believed in being self-sufficient. Most of all, she instilled in us a pride in "doing for ourselves." She would say, "We work for things, or we do without." She did ironing for a long time to help us have some things we needed. She helped out at Christmas especially.

She was very proud of our house, for it had been her home. I remember once when the creek was rising in a flash flood. A man from the fire department came in a boat and tried to rescue us, but she wouldn't leave the house. I was frightened and wanted to leave, but the more he pleaded the angrier she became. She finally lashed out at this white man who was concerned for us and said, "Get away from here, old nigger!" That term was the worst thing anybody could be called. I'll never forget her saying it. And I'll never forget how shocked I was the first time I saw it in print in Mark Twain's *Huckleberry Finn*. I never could like that book because, as a young schoolboy, I discovered that word in print. I didn't understand the reason.

Church was probably the most unifying place in our community for all of us. It still is, but I think it served an even stronger role then. All our hope was in God, who gave us purpose and direction in life. Everyone knew that. We were either Baptists or Methodists, and we all experienced the mystery of the way God came to us in the services. At my house there was another sacred mystery my grandmother handled. She baked the Communion bread on Saturday nights for Antioch Baptist Church, and we all had to stay out of the kitchen while she baked it. She would sit down, meditate, and pray while the bread was baking. I got to carry it down to church for her when she was finished. As I carried it, I always felt there was some sacredness in that bread.

Nothing that could happen in life was more important to us than what happened in church on Sundays. When the Spirit moved in the services, and people were happy, we felt God would be with us forever. It was comforting to see people blessed by God.

We went to church all day, a lot of times. There would be Sunday School, church, afternoon special programs, and the evening service. Sometimes we would go with Father to his country church, but Mother kept our membership at Antioch Baptist Church. To go there was to be a part of the

Poverty: Blessing in Disguise

community in a way we could never replace. That church and God belonged together in our young minds. Saturday nights, to get ready for Sunday, we all had to take our turn bathing in a wash tub.

I can't think of anything more helpful to us children than Sunday School. Those teachers put so much into teaching us about Christ. Their lessons became the basis for my faith in God. I never stopped going to Sunday School, even through my early married years when attendance so often drops off. By age seventeen, I had learned to tithe. Before that, at about age fourteen I had begun leading the songs in our church services. I think doing that showed me that God had some plan of greater leadership in mind for me. The Lord seemed to use the songs that I chose to bless people. They'd call out, and their happiness showed me the Lord was speaking to them. One of my favorite songs was, "Have You Any Rivers?" God specializes in things that seem impossible, the song says. I will never forget that song.

I remember my pastor's ability to pray. Rev. Bailey would talk to the Lord directly, conversationally, as if He were right in the room. Once when I was very sick, I remember him praying that the Lord would "do me as He did Hezekiah," and grant me fifteen more good years. At critical times in my life, I've remembered this prayer from my childhood pastor.

Some of the people who came to our church also left a permanent impression on me. We had several "peculiar" people—at least to our child's eyes. The church was open for all kinds of people. Rev. Price used to come sometimes. Some kids called him "Rev. Rear-back Price." He was a strange-looking man and his wife had deformed, fat hands, so they were quite an odd couple. Then there was Miss Mercy, a fat lady. She came in a horse and wagon while all the others came in cars. She drove the horse. Often an afflicted man came, too, his whole body flopping every time he took a step. Kids seemed to take a jeering attitude toward these folks, but I always felt sympathetic and became more deeply aware of others less fortunate than I.

Through all these early experiences in church, I kept thinking God would some day call me to do something special. I thought it was to be a lawyer, but looking back now, I see that the special effect the church services had on me should have showed me that God had something else in mind. When I grew older I avoided for a long time the possibility of a calling to the full-time ministry. I really delayed God's blessing by holding back. Knowing the sympathy for people that developed within me, and the joy I felt in church and Sunday school, I should have known that His calling was unavoidable.

I only know I'm thankful for those early years when we had so little to distract us from depending upon God alone for our livelihood and our happiness. Looking back on those times, I'd have to call them very rich preparation for all the difficult steps still to come. The path from childhood to adulthood is seldom easy, and we can thank God for every experience which keeps us faithful in the face of stress, doubt, pain, and confusion.

As I remember my small house, my loyal family, my father's leadership in directing our family devotions, and our neighborhood of love and support, I think we were some of the richest people ever to grow up in my town. God kept us dependent upon Him. I thank Him for that blessing.

6

Stress: It Brings Out the Tough Side of Faith

Stress is something we do to ourselves. We worry, make mistakes, walk away from God, and then think He has deserted us. Stress nearly tears us apart.

The stress I brought on myself, and that I allowed others to pile on me as I headed into adulthood, strained my faith to the breaking point. The confident belief which I had learned in childhood looked harder to me than I'd ever bargained for when I made my first profession of faith.

I began to fear I'd never reach any of the goals I'd set for myself. I think stress began killing me. In fact, my first serious bout of illness began after a time of severe stress.

It's taken me years to learn about managing stress—about letting God manage it for me. Since those first years of growing up, I've faced difficult decisions, trials of faith, and challenges to my health, my marriage, and my morality, without utterly falling. I've learned the hard way, but I've learned to manage stress. I nearly was crushed under its pressure before I found how great are God's resources for holding me up.

Today I know that no problem is too difficult for God. As I pray with people who come to me suffering from severe stress, I believe for them what they cannot believe for themselves—that God holds the healing for all our suffering. I see people in pain from things they've brought on themselves:

decisions they've made so unwisely, things they've done to their bodies and souls which they should never have attempted. And I see them suffering from the stress of strained relationships, the stress and hurt which others have caused in their lives. I wonder how all of us can fall down so many times. I am amazed at all the suffering and pain. Sometimes I'm tempted to despair when I hear the sad stories people bring to me.

But I've seen God intervene and bring healing to these lives too many times to allow that despair to take over—in me or in them. In fact, I've endured every kind of suffering and made every kind of mistake myself. That's why I know the power of God to lift all of us beyond despair. I've tested God so many times and found Him stronger than all my weakness. I know He has the way out of stress.

As I pray with people, I see them restored to faith and to peace of mind. I know only God can do that. And I know it is His promises and His powerful salvation in Christ which assures us of His continuing mercy to all of us, no matter how frail we are.

As a young adult, I found myself heading straight into more stress than I ever thought I could handle. As so often happens, my early mistakes were made in a time of enthusiasm for life and a sense that nothing could go wrong. I was still in high school at the time, in the old A. J. Moore High School which was torn down after the Waco high schools were integrated. During my tenth year of school I was voted "most versatile boy," and I was selected for the master's music honor society and competed in state drama and music competitions. Then I became president of the junior class, and everyone looked on me as a class leader.

I drove an old, raggedy car which all of us called the "green eye"; it had one green fender after an auto accident when my friend Allen forgot to look at the road for just a minute and sideswiped a parked car. We went to the scrap yard and found this green fender to replace the one he ruined after we paid for repair of the other car. It was all the fixing up we could afford. I have fond memories of that car, the good times with my friends, and the good times we all had in high school. My teachers were convinced I was headed for great things, and I was enthusiastic and determined to go to college.

But I was interested in courting the girls, too. Following the pattern of so many of my friends, I got a girl pregnant in my senior year. Somehow my friends had been able to shrug this problem off when it happened to them and remain friends with the girl but not marry her. I took my responsibilities too seriously to do that, even at this age, so I determined I should marry this girl and give my unborn child a name. My teachers and my family were terribly disappointed in me, and they also opposed my decision. They felt it would be the end of all my dreams, and that I was just adding one mistake to another. One teacher, Mr. Dickey, said I should always remember that a pencil has two ends—one to make a mistake and one to erase that mistake.

I was stubborn about my decision, though, and I determined to stick to principle. I realize how little I knew then about the hardships of life and how difficult things would be for us. But I think I would make the same decision again today anyhow. I believe in living by principle, no matter what the consequences. So I married Ernestine, and Evangeline René was born in August of 1960.

I was determined, despite my new responsibilities, to go to college at any cost. I'd been working at Reed's Flowers to support my family, earning twenty-seven to thirty dollars a week. I rented an apartment in the projects. I thought I was managing everything very well. But Ernestine was dissatisfied. When I started college, she felt she wanted to have more than I was able to provide. I felt she should be satisfied and stick by me. It didn't take us long to come to a complete division of minds. I was very disappointed and shaken. We were divorced when René was twenty months old. The failure of our marriage shattered me.

Worse than that, in my memory was the terrible scene that ended our relationship. My wife and I had ceased talking to each other entirely, simply living in the same house as strangers. I don't know how we endured that awful atmosphere. One evening she woke me up as I lay on the sofa and began a violent argument which became physically dangerous to us both. I try to blot it out of my mind now because I had never experienced anything like that, but it was so destructive we separated that night. I don't like to dwell on it, and I was very young then, but the fact that I have experienced this violence gives me compassion when other young couples come to me and tell me of their troubles. God can use even the ashes of our worst experiences to turn us toward the troubles of others.

I was less than twenty and had already ended the biggest failure of my life. That fact sent me into despair and bitterness. A little while after we separated in 1961, I had my first health breakdown by July, 1962. Doctors would say my illness was hereditary and bound to happen. But I know the way I handled stress was a major factor. I began to stay up all night to escape from the thought of my failure. I had begun to gamble and lead a life which I reject today. I was in school at the time, so I shouldn't have punished my body with bad habits the way I'd started to do. I began courting again, too, and I was on a date, sitting in a restaurant, when my ankle started to swell and my arthritis began. I had to

Stress: It Brings Out the Tough Side of Faith

be carried home, and that was the beginning of my long struggle up and down the mountain of ill health.

During that time I was studying at Paul Quinn College, and my faith had been weakened by what I was learning there, too, so I wasn't very strong in the faith when all this happened. I studied modern biology. When I learned about Neanderthal man, Java man, and all those other discoveries that seemed contradictory to what I had learned in church about creation, I began to question the Bible. I would go home and argue with my father about these things and upset him a lot. I was expressing a lot of anger and bitterness, I know.

I was wondering why God would allow the predicament that had developed in my life. By questioning whether God had really created the world, I was wondering if He had really created me. I wondered how God could be a loving God, so the more doubtful and bitter I became, the more I was unable to accept God's love for me. I must have been a rather unpleasant person to be around at that time because people began asking me if I had sinned. They treated me the way Job's friends treated him. I found very little comfort from anyone.

I became disillusioned with the church during that time, too. Today I know that the church, with all its difficulties, is still the church of God. I have seen Him do mighty works among His people in spite of all our imperfections.

As a youth, I began to focus on everyone's imperfections. I began to see them for the first time. There are things you don't see as young child, or even as a new Christian just discovering the church. At first, everything seems perfect and almost like heaven, and later on you find out that everybody is a long way from being perfect. I let my mind dwell on all the things that were wrong, and my bitterness increased.

The problem was that I had idealized so many of these people in my church while I was growing up. Suddenly, I saw people acting like dictators about the way they wanted the church to be run. I saw longtime members locked in power struggles. I saw people I had admired as saints doing some courting that they shouldn't have been doing because they were already married. I wondered why so many people I had admired so much did some of these things.

I was down in bed at my home for a long time while all these things were eating into my mind. My pain was unbearable, and my skin was beginning that peeling which is so hard for a young person to accept. I know my state of mind didn't help me at all. In his desperation, my father, although he was always a great man of faith, convinced me to try some things I really disapproved of. He and my family began to dabble in superstitious practices to free me. One time they went to a fortune teller who said to put a string in my bed and get me to drink some water from a place in Beaumont, Texas, where they had gone to ask for this advice. They did this, but they never told me where they got the idea because they knew I couldn't accept it.

Then after my first long stay in John Sealy hospital in Galveston—after the doctors had sent me home to die—Father took me to the "quack" doctor in Palestine, Texas, with the train engineer's cap. I remember him saying, "Yeah, Yeah. I see what's wrong," mixing up some stuff from pepper, mustard, and salt for my skin, and giving me vinegar. After two days, I decided this wouldn't work, so I rejected it. These visits and a few other things remind me of the lengths people will go to when they are not trusting God. Now that I've seen what God can do, I wonder why anyone places hope in such foolish measures as these.

Stress: It Brings Out the Tough Side of Faith

Father finally found a chiropractor named Ben Williams who gave me some relief from pain, and my first round of illness began to ease enough for me to return to school in 1964 after feeling I had been at death's door. As I look back, I realize how quickly I passed from the idealistic expectations of the growing up years to having to face the serious problems of adult life. We need to have our faith ready for whatever comes.

Even today I still know a lot of people with superstitious ideas. Back then, somebody hid a snake in my car one day, and I drove all the way to school before discovering it. People began saying that snake had "hoodooed" me, and that was why my skin was peeling like a snakeskin. They said it was punishment for my divorcing Ernestine. I think those comments show our insensitivity to a person who is going through suffering, no matter how it came about. I have no patience today with ideas like that.

I'm thankful that God strengthens us and sees us through the worst kinds of crises. I can testify to that. After my long bout with illness, my deep despair, and bitterness, I began to turn back to God and to health. I returned to Paul Quinn and felt I received some very good teaching to prepare me for life. Mrs. Barbara Elliot's English and speech courses, with discussion of regional dialects, made me more careful and conscious of the way I speak. When I later went to Baylor, a professor shocked me by saying, "You don't talk like a nigger." I really disliked what seemed to me a very rude comment, but I guess I have Mrs. Elliot to thank.

My vocabulary was good, too, because I began to read widely. I especially liked the Greek mythology that I studied in Miss Bobbye Moore's class, and I also began to read newsmagazines all the time. People later told me I talked "over their heads," and I had to learn to simplify my vocabulary again. I had a lot of appreciation for Dr. Vivienne Mayes's math course, and for Dr. Andy Moore, a white professor from Baylor who came over to Paul Quinn to teach us. He showed a lot of personal interest in disadvantaged young people. Paul Quinn College, which had only black students, was a very affirming experience and a good way to begin my education.

I thought I could transfer to Baylor University and continue to make the good grades I had made at Quinn. I was in for a disappointment. I found the work at Baylor very difficult, and I decided I was about two years behind everyone else in academics and in cultural advantages. I think our black young people still face that lag a lot of times, though not so much as I did. I just hadn't had all the outside experiences, travel, and other advantages of these Baylor students, and I had not grown up surrounded with books and other stimulation. Of course, I felt very isolated at Baylor, too. I was one of two black students there, and one of the first two to receive a Baylor degree. So I pretty much had to get along by myself, even though by the time I graduated there were about thirteen black students.

It was a lonely experience, but I had opened myself up again to God, and He was beginning to bless me. I saw that my bitterness had taken me to a dead end in life, and I was seeking for ways to answer my questions about faith that would allow me to go forward again. God was very gracious, as He always is. He simply wants us to stop fighting and seek for His ways. We will find them.

I found some of the answers I sought right in the Baylor classrooms. God used several courses I was taking to reassure me.

While still at Paul Quinn, before transferring to Baylor, I'd taken a survey of the Old and New Testaments, and I

Stress: It Brings Out the Tough Side of Faith

began to look at Christ differently. He seemed more real and historical after my study, and I also began to understand the fall of man. We had sinned from the beginning, and that was how things had gotten so badly off the track, I saw. Somehow that explained a lot of my trouble to me. In my thinking, I began tilting things back again. In thinking of the problem of how old the earth was, I realized that time can be calculated differently. So I was more comfortable with the Bible and my difficulties with Genesis. I saw that the biblical emphasis was on saving souls and not on giving a history of the world.

In thinking of Jesus, I was impressed with a Baylor professor who talked about the "overwhelming evidence" for the historical Jesus. That thought kept me on track in terms of Jesus. Dr. Jack Flanders and Dr. Dan McGee and others in the Baylor religion department helped me to begin jelling things back together to give me a better understanding of the biblical viewpoint. My faith was never really shaken anymore after that. My mind was settled.

At the same time, I began to be involved again in church and in song leading. I began to consider some kind of ministry more seriously as I considered what God wanted me to do with my life. I had made my mistakes, I had suffered a lot already, and I wanted my life to count for something for God. At that time I saw my life taking on a prophetic role, rather than a preaching role. I felt a calling to the needs of people and to injustice. I felt that everything I was doing by being in school and by involvement in church was God directed. My pain had completely left me and I considered that a miracle after I had suffered so long and much. I was a little stiff, but I did not consider myself a handicapped person in any way. I allowed no one to open doors for me or show me any special favors. I felt confident, with God at work in my life.

After passing through so many trials and being restored to health and belief through the mercy of God, I began to ask God for specific direction for my life. As a result, He led me to acknowledge my call publicly to the ministry in the spring of 1966 while still a student at Baylor. At first I'd wanted my father to tell me how to recognize when you have a calling. He never would tell me. I remember getting into my car, going out to the lake, and sitting there, thinking about it. I still went to dances at the club, and things like that. But I began to feel I was in the wrong place everytime I went. I felt like Jacob wrestling with the angel. I had been helping my father out in his churches, so I was getting a real feeling for ministry and for preaching, but I also still felt I was headed for law school. In church, I often sang the song, "Have You Any Rivers?" That song always inspired me even more to seek God's will. I had crossed so many rivers by God's grace.

I finally crossed the most important river—accepting God's call in my life—because I saw I would only be happy and whole and at peace with myself when I did so. I came very close to accepting that call at age twenty-two while my brother Sam was preaching at Second Baptist Church in Waco in a revival service. In one of those services, I knew without doubt that the Lord had something definite in ministry for me to do. The theme of Sam's sermon was: "If a man die, shall he live again?" Those words touched me. I'd been so close to death already in my young life, and I knew what it was like to despair of life and hope mentally, too. I'd tried all the vain things of life and found how hollow they were. Nothing but God would satisfy me. I must serve Him according to His will, I knew without a doubt.

But even so, I delayed acknowledging my calling for four more years. I don't know what was holding me back, but I was dragging my feet.

Stress: It Brings Out the Tough Side of Faith

Not until 1966 did I acknowledge my calling and tell people publicly of God's hand upon me. After more spells of serious illness, I knew God was trying to get my full commitment. When I accepted His call, I felt the burdensome worry and uncertainty I had carried for so long roll off my shoulders.

For some time, I felt I could preach and still be a lawyer. God allowed me to hold that dream for awhile, because it was the one which had given me such purpose and direction all through my school years. I didn't know that even that goal would later be turned aside for another one, but I knew God would direct me, whatever happened. Today I know that every high hope we have of doing God's will is fulfilled in us somehow. Though I am not a lawyer, I am an advocate of my people in whatever condition I find them. God has fulfilled my desire to serve, but in His own better way.

I suffered some disappointments shortly after accepting my calling, and the way I handled them may have led to a relapse in my health. Just because I had taken that step didn't guarantee that from then on everything would be perfect. I think that's an illusion we all have. We think God should suddenly spare us the trials of becoming mature by making everything else easy for us.

It has taken me a long time to learn that disappointments are God's way of pointing me in a better direction. While I was at Baylor I was asked to be a leader in the new Upward Bound program. The program was designed to help minority young people upgrade their skills at an early enough age that they could succeed when it came time to go to college. I thought I was to have a major leadership role in designing this program and I was very excited about it. But I never was given any real responsibility, so I spent most of my time in the program feeling very frustrated and passed over. I think

I let that feeling eat away at me. At the same time, I began to question whether my goal to get to law school was realistic. I'd lost more time from school due to another round of ill health, and I found myself unprepared when it came time to take the law-school entrance exam. I went through a period of despair at the loss of my dream.

I know now I shouldn't have let that disappointment affect me the way it did. God has never left my side as He has worked out His plans in my life. I wish I could tell all young people who want to follow the will of God that nothing can keep God from performing His work within them. Disappointments are no sign that God has left us. In fact, God is probably working out something better for us, if we could only see that.

I discovered, to my surprise, that God wanted to use my skills to become a teacher. These same skills have helped me in my ministry today. When I reached my last semester at Baylor, the question came up about where to place me for student teaching since I was the first black teacher's candidate at the university. The professors accepted the suggestion of Barry Thompson, a progressive young assistant superintendent in Waco, to place me in Tennyson Junior High School, then an all-white school. I accepted the challenge and discovered that I was quite able to handle it. That was a very affirming realization: I was not only equal to the challenge of an all-white world, but I actually had something to offer these young people. When I graduated, the school system showed they liked my work by asking me to stay on.

I remember some very stimulating times in my classes, urging these young people to really think about social and political issues. I felt right at home doing what God had given me to do. I never felt inferior or inadequate, and I thanked God for all the academic experiences and trials of life that had prepared me for this opportunity. Here I was in a situation that could have been considered very stressful, and I felt God undergirding me completely and giving me a great deal of peace.

I was still living at home while I was a teacher, and I began to see my father suffer with ill health. We were "running pretty good" together and I had come to respect his wisdom and spiritual leadership as I worked with him. I had been taking Father to the doctor quite a bit because he was having trouble getting his breath. He'd had five or six heart attacks. I like to think of all the times I heard him preparing his sermon in the little back room in our house. I'd hear him start to hum after a while; then I knew that the Spirit had begun its work, and the sermon was really underway.

Early one morning as my sister and I were both getting up to go to work, we heard him call out, "Lord, have mercy!" He had dropped to his knees. My sister and I were holding him up on each side and we couldn't get him up. A puff of air came from his mouth and he was dead, just like that. It took me a long time to get that picture out of my mind. His funeral was the largest I had ever seen at Antioch Church. Country preachers had come to him for years to ask him to prepare sermons for them and to ask his advice about so many things. These rural preachers called him the "R.F.D. Dean." His studious, well-prepared messages have been a model for me. He really knew homiletics, even though he had only gone through the tenth grade. He had spent his life studying on his own.

Losing someone close to us is a very difficult experience. We don't like to think about it. But sometimes we have to face up to it. We need to learn how to grieve properly and then to use that person's best qualities to inspire us as we go about our own work. I think often of my father's humming or whistling in that back room, and I recognize that certain feeling he was having of the Spirit being with him. There is a certain feeling I connect with the Lord. When I get that signal, it stays with me through my sermon preparation, and clear through until the Sunday services. I'm thankful God makes it possible for us to talk and communicate directly with Him.

God began preparing me for even greater challenges of stress than I had yet imagined, as He directed me toward taking up leadership in my community and in my father's two churches after his death. Now as I look back, I see that none of the hard times I endured were wasted. Because I allowed God to take my life and set it on track and because I set aside the bitterness I had felt as a young man, I have found the strength to go on through the really tough challenges of life. I've faced misunderstanding, failure, health breakdown, and frustration. But I've seen God take me through every circumstance. I've learned to walk into every new situation without fear because God is with me—strengthening me and supporting me.

If we can use our stress to let God take over our lives, we'll learn to be tough servants of the Lord. I think that's what God would like to do with us—make us tough enough to serve Him in every circumstance. Because He comes to us through the Holy Spirit to bring us His special grace, nothing should be too hard for us if He calls us to do it. That's what He continues to show me, even today when I endure great pain and weakness. I can ignore stress, through prayer, because I know God can do with us many things, far beyond anything we can ask or think (see Eph. 3:20). I remind myself again and again that "my strength is made perfect in weakness" (2 Cor. 12:9). As I pass through every stressful situation, God increases my endurance and my faith becomes stronger. He is faithful.

7
Rejection: God Honors Our Courage

Rejection is always painful. It hurts the most when the rejection comes as a result of things we did for the best of reasons. Rejection is one of the hazards of leadership. Anyone who takes God seriously and wants to step out and act upon the commitment of faith is likely to experience some rejection.

I've experienced a lion's share of this rejection, sometimes for things I could have done differently and other times because people did not understand my intentions. A person who takes the risk of leadership stands where everyone else can see. Naturally there will be disagreement about the choices we make. Of course, not everyone will think we are doing the right thing. Even if our acts are done in the name of God, we have no guarantee that He would do exactly as we are doing. Yet we must believe God will both guide us and correct our mistakes because we are acting in obedience to His spirit.

We have to hold our heads high and keep on. At least people will be able to say of us that we tried, rather than that we stood still and did nothing while needs, hurting, and pain lay all around.

Ever since my adolescence, I believed God was going to do something with my life to help others. I think God sometimes gives us those early dreams to prepare us for what He has for us later. By sixth grade I had determined to be a lawyer and help my people. In high school I realized I had leadership gifts as a result of my work in student government. Teachers and others began telling me I would be a leader if I did not waste my life with foolish mistakes. I knew, as others have told me they also knew, that God would do something with me.

I did not realize at that time the cost of leadership. The hard lessons of leadership come to us gradually. In that respect, God is merciful. He calls us first, and then as we are ready to bear it, we learn the hazards of our call. I think the call to exercise leadership is unavoidable, once we open ourselves up to the claim of God upon our lives.

The only way to avoid taking responsibility is to avoid God. I did that for a few years, but once I realized that the only path to a full life was with God, I stopped resisting Him. At that point, I was ready to take up whatever He had for me.

My illness never stood in the way of my responding to God's call. Sometimes I would be down in bed for a few weeks or even months, but I would always return with a fresh desire to serve. Those times seemed to strengthen my resolve rather than weaken it. God would give me some fresh vision of what He wanted to do with my life as I recovered from my health failures.

Leadership causes a lot of stress, I've found. Some of my friends and family say that the stress I encountered as I tried to do some things for my people made my health worse than it would have been. But I say to them that I could do nothing else than what I have done. To stop living the life I believed God had for me would have been disastrous. My doctor today tells me that it was my activity and my resolve to be well so I could serve that saw me through the worst of times.

Rejection: God Honors Our Courage

"Other people would have died from your health problems," Dr. Lea said to me recently, "but you were determined to live. Your determination kept you going."

I'm thankful today for the doctor's confirmation that I was doing the right thing. I would do everything again today that I have done, given the choice. I only wish I could have known then some of the things I know now—especially that following God's call is the path to inner peace.

One of the biggest problems I had to deal with as a leader was bitterness. When we step out and decide to seek change and justice, sometimes we feel overwhelmed with the wrong we see. I had carried with me for a long time a bitterness about the way things are in our society. I saw the inequality that black people lived with day in and day out. I felt that I resented it a lot more than many of them did. They often wished I would not be so vocal about it because I made them uncomfortable.

While we were still in school, I had trouble saying the pledge to the flag because I felt the things we were saying in there weren't true for the people I cared about. So when we came to the phrase about "liberty and justice for all," I would whisper the phrase, "for all white people." That really upset my friends, but I couldn't help it then. It was a matter of integrity with me.

Later on, when I was involved in court cases, we all had to stand up when the judge entered, and I had trouble standing up for one of the judges because I knew he was a racist. I did so reluctantly because I knew the court proceedings would not go on if I refused. But I always felt that principles about right and wrong were more important than compromises. I never felt that I could compromise about anything.

My refusal to compromise caused a lot of trouble for me

and for others. I regret any misunderstandings my positions may have caused, but I still think my integrity was at stake in so many issues. I couldn't adopt the attitude of so many that if I would just make concessions, I would get some of what I sought. I felt what I was asking for was too important to make those kinds of concessions. Today there are still people who don't think I acted wisely. They think of me as an angry and bitter person. Many of the people who read the newspapers and watched television during the 1970s have the impression that I am still a bitter and angry person. When they hear my name they say, "Oh, Robert Gilbert? It's too bad about him. He really caused so much trouble and he was so eaten up with bitterness. Is he still that way?"

I want to say to them that I am no longer bitter and angry. God has taken that from me and given me a spirit of love and forgiveness toward those whom I genuinely felt were not dealing fairly with me. I am not bitter toward them and not bitter toward God. I am known as a rather gentle person when I am acting in love toward those who are in need. I still have that side of me that refuses to compromise. I think God requires of everyone the very best that is within them. I advocate 100-percent Christianity, just as I advocated 100-percent justice during my period of community involvement.

But today I have learned the lesson of Scripture that says, "Let not the sun go down upon your wrath," and "Be ye angry, and sin not" (Eph. 4:26). God has taught me never to go to sleep with unresolved anger. I end each day with a spirit of forgiveness toward anyone who has caused me pain or whose actions I cannot understand. This new attitude has brought me peace in my heart as never before.

A difficult thing I found about leadership is the way it saps your energy and your prayer life. When you are involved in

Rejection: God Honors Our Courage

a controversy or are seeking to make changes in community structures, you can become so busy and so caught up in what is happening that you don't have time to withdraw and pray. I felt this lack many times, yet because I was working as well as trying to serve my community, I was very pressed for time. All I can say today is that I believe prayer is the essential element in any lasting changes God intends to make. I would try even harder to find time for prayer, and I would understand even more clearly our absolute dependence upon God.

If you are called to community leadership, you have to know that God has led you into it if you are to have peace about it. So many things happen to stretch your patience that without God it is easy to give up. During the 1970s I felt that I was called to a ministry similar to the ideals left to us by Martin Luther King, Jr. I patterned my ministry after him, dealing with issues without injecting any violence, and going in the name of the Lord to raise the consciousness of people who needed to be changed. I always felt the Lord was with me in whatever I was doing. I went into so many situations without fear. I don't think anybody is ever wrong in the final sense of that word if God is with them. That conviction kept me from being afraid when things began to happen that frustrated me.

Today, I still feel called to community leadership. Because I don't have the energy that I used to have to work both in the community and in the church, I have had to make choices. It is within the church that I see the most hope, so I have put my talents there. But I still feel that someone must prayerfully play the role of the prophet to our society today; someone must show people what they must do to bring about greater justice.

I feel called today to call others into leadership. I believe that the church must supply leadership, if the world around us is to be changed for the better. I don't believe in sitting back and waiting for heaven. I want to urge my people to accept God's call in their own lives and to step out and do whatever they can to help in some way. Truly, the harvest is plentiful. I receive calls every day about people who are in trouble or suffering in some way. It is more than I can handle on my own, and I only wish and pray that many others would respond to the call of God to leadership and would move out into the world to do whatever they can. The laborers are few. We need so many more of them.

When I was most involved in the community, I felt my involvement was a form of ministry—a prophetic form, just as my ministry today is a preaching form. Faith gave me no fear of death, despite threats that came to me while I was on the school board. I received threatening phone calls, a bomb threat, and my house was burned out during one tense controversy. I was home alone at the time of the fire and I got myself out safely. The incident was said to be "of suspicious origin," but it was never even reported in the newspaper. I always felt that was wrong. Yet through all the most heated times of confrontation in a town which was just beginning to change, I never feared for my life. I felt committed to die for the cause, and I felt strongly led by God to go all the way. I envisioned somebody like Amos going to the government and saying, "Let justice roll down like waters" (5:24, RSV). I felt God sent me to deal with whatever was wrong. That conviction controlled me from 1968-78, eleven years in all.

I think the Lord prepared me for my involvement in the community during my years of schooling. I became observant of the larger world through my reading in newsmagazines and editorials, and I began to think critically and read closely. During one class at Baylor I read Senator Fulbright's "The Arrogance of Power," and that set me to thinking.

Rejection: God Honors Our Courage

During the 1960s so many things were happening in our cities—so much upheaval between the races. I was confused about where our country was heading. I watched closely the way Dr. Martin Luther King, Jr., operated—with never any violence at all. I was deeply distressed when both King and Robert Kennedy were killed.

On the day of King's funeral, I put a television set in front of my class at Tennyson Junior High where I was teaching. Some of the students were interested, but others were not. The *Waco Citizen,* a family-run newspaper in our town, said that King deserved to die. I wrote a blistering reply, and several came to me to ask my true feelings, including my principal, Mr. Herman Thomas. I tried to make them understand how much I thought our society needed to change.

A group of concerned citizens formed a study group to discuss some of these issues. I was invited to join. We called it the Doris Miller Dialogue Group and we spent several sessions talking. Out of that group came some ideas that gave me hope.

The first effort I was involved in following this study group was the Human Relations Commission, formed in 1968. As a member of that commission I made my "public debut." I hoped that commission could help to bring about real change in my town. But I soon saw that the commission had no "teeth" to really implement change. It became a talk session with no power to solve anything. That agency became my forum for the next three years to say what I thought needed to be changed. When we were sworn into office on the commission, I immediately walked to the stand and told the city council publicly that they had created a commission with no power to act upon issues in a concrete manner, in spite of all our requests. Because I took that position publicly, asking for guidelines to be set up for the commission and asking for subpoena power, so we could really gather information that would help us in our work, I began to receive the image in the media of being negative and radical. From that time on, I found myself always in confrontation with the people in power in the city. My only goal was to achieve justice.

I felt those in power thought I should be more subservient to them. I addressed them as if we were on exactly the same level, and that made them feel I was abrasive. They said I could get more accomplished if I would come to them in a supplicating attitude. I could not do that. I served for one term on the commission, but I was not appointed to a second term. Several of the other members returned to serve again, including former mayors Joe L. Ward, P. M. Johnson, and prominent citizens Jack Kultgen, Rabbi Mordecai Podet, Dr. W. C. Perry of Baylor, Mrs. Ross Sams, and several others.

Within the next three years I found the real arena where I felt God had called me to make some changes. That was in our city schools. My background had prepared me for this. I was the first black graduate of Baylor University and the first black teacher in an all-white junior high school. As a teacher, I spent all my daytime in a white world, and I felt I understood its patterns. I developed a respect for promptness of time, learned a business sense, and learned to understand the importance of keeping records. As a teacher I had learned to stand toe to toe and examine public issues with the brightest students in Waco. I realized that the only way to deal with issues is to do research—to have facts and figures ready before beginning to talk. That research, which is so necessary if you are to be a public figure, is what I was prevented from pursuing as a member of the Human Relations Commission. I knew, and I still know, that you cannot make changes until you have done your homework. You must begin with facts and you must have access to the sources of those facts. You have to know what you are talking about.

By 1971 I began to take a close look at Waco's school situation and to make some allegations. I was asked to meet with people from Washington, DC, who came down to investigate those allegations. Waco was to have been integrated beginning in the early 1960s on a grade-by-grade basis. But by 1970, we saw that this was not taking place. After the federal government investigated, Waco schools were integrated by court order in 1972-73 for the first time. I knew it would be difficult for everybody. My wife and I and some other concerned citizens tried to form some discussion groups among black and white high school students to talk together and begin to come to some liking and understanding. We did this on a very small scale, but it worked well.

I have always believed that if we could have had more of this we could have solved many problems through communication. I have always felt that if white and black parents could have come together more often to talk about their concerns, they could have helped the schools to get through the most difficult days. I think the parents should have been involved in what was taking place in the classrooms from the very first. I've always felt badly that they weren't. I think black parents could have insisted on some things that would have made it easier for the teachers. But when I proposed these suggestions I found that the people making the decisions in Waco were not interested in my views and wanted to press on with their own plans.

I still wish we could have consulted together and worked together.

To my dismay, I felt myself in a combative position. The

district came up with a four-sector plan in which black children were bused for eleven years of school, and white children were bused only to the sixth-grade centers. That situation and some other points caused me to work with Bishop Adams of the A.M.E. Church, then at Paul Quinn College. We founded an organization called the Black Federation, with six-hundred to eight-hundred people gathered at the college to discuss integration problems. We represented thirty-nine to forty black organizations in Waco, as one united group. The community seemed to fear this federation because we met so massively.

I became a primary plaintiff in integration and served as a witness in Waco and in Austin. At the beginning of school I asked for a one-day boycott on school registration because we felt the plan placed the burden of busing on the black community. But this symbolic boycott, which was only to last for one day as a kind of public statement, caused confusion and division among blacks. The police parked in front of my office at the Bledsoe-Miller Center on the river. We set up freedom centers that day for the children to come to. But of all the black children in Waco, only four hundred to five hundred turned up, so I felt the effort was a failure.

Nevertheless, I had begun to take some leadership in seeking change in Waco, and I eventually found myself asked to run for election to the school board in 1976. Several others in the black community who were asked to run declined, not wishing to be involved in controversy. I had no fear of doing what was necessary. After my election, I was very disappointed that the three white members of the board and their families left the room while I was being administered the oath of office.

During all my nearly three years on the board, I always felt I was on the outside. I believed that decisions we were to make at board meetings had actually been made at early

Rejection: God Honors Our Courage

morning breakfast or coffee sessions, and these were things I was never invited to join. The members would show up with their strategies all outlined in their minds, and I became a spectator to their decisions. So I had to develop some strategies of my own which involved selecting some key issues and researching them thoroughly so I would have some leverage in terms of knowing what I was talking about.

A number of times I warned the school board about illegal kinds of meetings and agreements. In our closed sessions we were only supposed to deal with personnel issues. But they would hold full meetings discussing many public issues without the public there. I refused to participate.

When issues regarding the progress in integration came up, as they often did, I tried to have solid research to support what we were talking about. I used the statistics the school system had available. I was concerned about the tracking of black students into special education classes, which still kept them segregated from the white students. I would go to the schools during lunch, sit in the cafeteria, talk to the students, and try to understand what was happening to them. Then I would walk down the halls during classes, and I would see a white class in one room and a black class in another. I felt integration was not really working. I wanted to work with teachers and parents to see how this could be changed.

I felt the school board was more concerned with other issues than with education in the 1970s. They wanted to build a sports complex with Baylor and the city, and I thought they were more concerned about athletics than about teaching. I always tended to side with the concerns of the teachers in an issue, and I felt the board was completely disinterested in the problems of the teachers and in academic improvement. When I would raise this thought, they would say that sports were important because "leadership involves leading teams." I didn't hear anything about "getting the maximum out of children," which was my chief concern. Instead, I felt the board was generally negative about the concerns teachers would bring to them, and I heard them belittle these concerns privately, showing a lack of respect for issues of teachers as a group.

I was shocked at the money spent on the school-board members in one way or another. Our board meetings were always preceded by sumptuous meals for board members and key administrators. At those dinners I usually felt alone because people tended not to want to talk to me. One of the administrators in town was black, and I felt he was uncomfortable about talking with me, so I usually ended up by myself. He didn't want to have difficulty with the people he was working with, I thought, so I didn't want to put him on the spot.

I regretted the fact that blacks employed by the school district avoided me in public. They seemed to fear for their jobs. They would speak to me in church and sometimes open their hearts to me, telling me of their concerns. But being in public with me was another matter. I always felt the black community held back from taking an active hand in public issues because they or their spouses were employed in the schools, or they worked as domestics or in businesses of prominent white people, and they didn't want to jeopardize their employment. At any rate, I was a maverick and a source of discomfort to them.

The school-board members took a trip to Anaheim, California, one time. We were supposed to be going out there to a national association of school-board members. I was amazed that the trip was actually like a big party, with seemingly little school-administration business being transacted. Some of the board members felt embarrassed because they sensed I thought the meeting had turned into sort

Rejection: God Honors Our Courage

of a party. I began to have my doubts about the board's being able to shape serious school policy.

While we were in Anaheim, I was invited to preach in a church, and my theme was: "Christ Is my 'Anyhow' Savior." In spite of everything, He came from the grave *anyhow,* and you, I, and everyone can make it in this life *anyhow.* I felt those words were very relevant to the stress I was feeling in my efforts to exercise leadership and responsibility.

I was never able to effect much change in the schools in terms of the academic program and getting help for black children who had fallen behind in their lessons. That made me very unhappy. I worried about children who had been tracked into lower-ability classes. I thought they would be trapped there the rest of their lives unless some serious remedial efforts were mandated. I knew the teachers couldn't do it all, without the support of the board. I tried to gather information on that, and I always felt blocked. I also tried to bring attention to the discipline problems in the schools. I felt the number of black students suspended, compared to the number of suspended white students, was way out of proportion. I wanted the board to look at the problem and come up with some solutions. I could get nowhere with this problem, even though I was willing to work with the board to see what might be done. They wanted to prevent me from gathering the statistics to pursue it. This was one more instance of my feeling blocked from gathering the information I needed.

Once when I tried to gather information, the board told me I could no longer have access to the records. I wrote the attorney general about their action. He ruled in my favor. But the board then said I owed them four-hundred dollars for the information. I refused, of course. By that time I was getting close to the end of my tenure, so I took a hard position on this issue.

I was able to get some changes in personnel practices, so I felt my time on the board had been of help in some way. I only wish it could have been even more helpful. I did convince the board to change the pay scale for maids and cooks. They usually were not hired full-time, so they didn't have any benefits, and they worked at a low hourly wage. During the summer they had no pay. We increased their wages from $2.50 to $3.75 an hour for those with seniority, and we spread their pay out over twelve months.

I also asked the board to come up with an affirmative-action plan for hiring. I had all the facts on hiring procedures, so I knew some plan was needed. On this issue, and also in the issue of discipline in the schools, I had carefully gathered my information. I went to the media to get their attention on these issues. But whenever they reported my views in the news, they always said I "alleged" something, rather than that I had presented researched facts.

I felt the media needed to be more responsible in the way they reported things about me since I had the facts to back up my positions. So I went to the folks at the *Tribune Herald* and showed them an article I felt was unfair. I said, "Print the facts and reject this negative image." They accused me of always being "racial." I said, "These are facts. Look them up, print them, and stop the negativism." I looked out into the newsroom, and I did not see a single black employee, so I asked about it. This made matters worse and ended our visit.

During my time on the board, I realized I could do little to make active changes since I was usually voting alone. So I used my time to raise public consciousness, hoping that in time others would come onto the board who would change the voting balance and begin to deal with these serious

Rejection: God Honors Our Courage

issues. I still think education is a student-teacher-administrator-board-parent issue. Everyone needs to be involved.

After two and one-half years of anguish and stress, I finally resigned from the board without filling my six-year term. I resigned over the selection of a coach. Once more the board was dealing with an athletic issue rather than an academic one, but I felt justice needed to be done in this case. The candidates for the position included two white coaches and one minority candidate. One of the white candidates pulled out. When the coach was selected, the black candidate was never given consideration, even though many of Waco's athletes were black, and I felt the city needed a black coach. I called a press conference and asked black people to boycott all sports. They refused to support me, saying they feared losing athletic scholarships and opportunities. That distressed me because I didn't see very many of our young people getting those scholarships anyway at the time, so I felt there was little to lose by the boycott. I felt I was at cross-purposes with them. If my own people would not stand with me when their interests were at stake, I felt I could no longer serve. So I resigned.

I felt very alone. I had suffered so many things on behalf of my people, and I knew they didn't understand all my actions. But the fact that they were beginning to turn from me and say I was hurting their public image was more than I could bear. I felt I had no other recourse than to resign. When I think of all that today, I still feel very sad. I'm not sure people understood how much pain I went through to bring about some good.

Today I'm willing to say I should have stuck with the school board rather than to resign. At the time, I didn't think

I had any other choice. I still think community involvement is part of what it is to be a servant of Christ.

As I look back over the events in Waco during the past fifteen years, I realize that I have been involved in some way in almost every push for improvement among black people. My work on the school board was only one part of that overall movement which took place during the 1970s for black people to come into their heritage in this country. It was a slow and painful process, and I think I was involved during the time that change was most difficult for everyone. I'm thankful that God made me willing to take on the pain and the risk. I wouldn't have wanted it any other way. There is no better life than a life offered up for one's friends, in the name of service to Christ and through His redemptive power. Everything I did was attempted in that spirit. I may have seemed impatient: I know I was. But I was always seeking God's best in what I attempted for Him.

At the beginning of the 1970s, our efforts for community harmony began with dialogue with some key leaders in Waco. Jarrell McCracken of Word, Inc., encouraged a group of black leaders to talk with white leaders. Among us were Cullen Harris, Ulysses Cosby, Willie Hobbs, and Thurman Dorsey from my community and Dan McGee, Malcolm Duncan, Jamie Anderson, Jesse Derrick, V. M. Cox, and Cullen Smith from Waco's elite. We talked about basic issues first, and then about specifics. When it came to the need for more jobs for blacks, these Waco leaders said they would hire more blacks if they could find well-qualified applicants.

So I set up a talent bank—a school for developing skills. They set up a program called Association for Selective Career Opportunities (ASCO) to hire me to do that. Blacks were to give me the names of potential applicants for skilled positions. Whites were to give me entree into the business

Rejection: God Honors Our Courage

world. I was supposed to help employers set up affirmative-action programs and to counsel minorities about interviewing and professionalism on the job. I was excited the first year and did begin to get some minority applicants through the door. By the end of the five-year effort, I had seen over five-hundred applicants successfully placed in jobs, including one engineer, the first anchorperson on television station KWTX, and the first reporter on the *Tribune Herald.*

But some of the men who had promised to help the most never came through with their own hiring. When some of us managed to get a program called Minority Forum on television to discuss public issues, I discovered that the program was continually moved around and never given a permanent place on the schedule. I felt a lack of commitment and an avoidance of unpleasant issues from those whose help I needed.

I became concerned especially with the public's hiring record. They seemed to me to be a target for complaint as opposed to private businesses. They were responsible to the public for what they did. I didn't see any blacks working in government-paid offices. So I filed a suit with the EEOC. I used letterhead stationery of ASCO to file that complaint, and the people on the board convinced me I had made a mistake.

I was also involved in action to help black women who had completed the RN program at the community college to pass their state board exams. They needed developmental courses, and I worked with the president of McLennan Community College to see this program implemented. I also went to the state police and learned what was necessary for black applicants to be accepted into the program and to survive the rigors of training. I was invited to Austin to speak at state police headquarters, and I talked about the need for more sensitivity all around. I soon saw the state become more aggressive in putting blacks onto the force.

I also was able to intervene in a case of some black teachers, including my sister-in-law, who were told they would not receive a teaching contract. The reason given was their discipline problems. I went to the school board with another minister, and we gave the board quite a challenge. I felt teachers having trouble should be helped, rather than suspended. Another time I had suggested that teachers be given remedial help if there was some question about their work. The school board reversed their decision after I intervened. I was always troubleshooting in situations like these.

I have every reason for encouragement from these and other gains. For a time I worked with Paul Quinn College in job placement, too, and saw several good applicants placed in jobs. I split my time between the college and the public sector in working on hiring. I felt I helped to make the community more sensitive to hiring and to opening doors for black people. I began to be called frequently to mediate in tough situations, including court cases, school suspension cases, and many difficult events. I was always glad to be of help.

Naturally, I met with some people and situations that I regret. I took on the cause of six to eight young men who appeared to be hoodlums, but who wanted to set up a breakfast program for the needy. I supported these young men and got funds for them, but some of the men were crooked in their dealings, and the program failed.

I helped a group of black Muslims for a while, for I felt we were working for the same improvements. I supported them in developing their grass-roots newspaper. But I soon discovered that when I would write anything for them that had Christian sentiments, they would refuse to use it, or

Rejection: God Honors Our Courage

they would change it. I felt they were driving a wedge in the black community and causing a lot of trouble for my credibility by what they were doing. They began to attack everybody in the community. Finally, the *Waco Citizen* printed a story that I was the grass-roots leader of this group. I think people believed that for a long time even though I had only tried to be of help in an effort which later turned on me. I couldn't sue or ask for a retraction from the newspaper because I was a public leader.

I have simply had to live with misunderstanding. I think there are still some people today who believe the things they read about me in the newspapers. I wish they could have talked to me in person, so I could have explained the real circumstances. I think they might have understood me, had they known what my real actions and purposes were. I'd like people to have understood that I was acting in obedience to Christ and not for anything I might gain. It was not a comfortable way to live to stand up so many times and to ask for change. I felt I had to do it as a matter of principle and of faith.

I would say to anyone today who is faced with such a leadership calling that we must have a love that is superlative. We can't love a little. We must love to the degree that Christ loved.

To have this genuine love, we must pray constantly. I once feared God would condemn me for my negative attitudes toward those who stood in my way. I had a negativism that drew the line on who I would love. I felt those who opposed me were working for the devil sometimes. But five or six years ago, I came to a better understanding. I became more trusting and accepting of all people, not on the basis of race but of individuals. I think that breakthrough in my attitude saved me from despair. I am living today with a redemptive attitude.

I left the school board with some bitterness, but as I turned more to my work within the church I began to see that many of my goals for my people could be realized within the church. I began a tutoring program for young children. I encouraged my people to be concerned for the poor, the needy, the ill, and the aged. The church must always be a place where people of all stations in life can come together and find their needs met.

As I began to give all my experiences in leadership over to the Lord, I felt Him continually taking the anger and bitterness from me. I feel within me that God made me a more loving person.

I can identify with Christ who had so many rejections. He still reached out in love. I've had disappointments, misunderstandings, and lived with things I knew were not right. I remember that Christ endured far more than that. I take Him as my example. I take Him as my source of strength. His Spirit has worked within my life to confirm His calling in my heart and to say to me that all is well. He will always honor the risk, the pain, and the courage that it took to act in His name. I must leave everything in His hands and be thankful for the privilege of leadership.

8

His Eye Is on the Sparrow: And I Know He Watches Me

Every Sunday morning I sing the song, "His Eye Is on the Sparrow, and I Know He Watches Me." God has kept my life from falling and has brought me back to something better and more meaningful at the end of each difficult time. God's purposes for my life are coming together now as never before, though my health is always fragile. Though I will never understand His mercy entirely, I see God's renewing power in the church and in lives all around me. None of it is perfect, but we have a God who can never fail.

I claim the promise that I can do all things through Christ who strengthens me. In my spirit I have never been so sure of God's promise to sustain me, even though I have never had less physical strength than I do now. God needs only our obedience and our love to do everything He needs with us.

I know that, because I have seen this church grow from sixty to three-hundred members. I have been at Carver Park Baptist Church in Waco, Texas, since 1978. In all that time I have been seriously ill as much as I have been well, and by the mid-1980s, I gave in to a wheelchair. My energy and desire to serve God are as strong as they ever were. And He has produced miracles in my life to keep me here in this church serving these people I love so well.

Something God has placed within me makes all my physical circumstances fade away in a few minutes after I arrive at this church. I see His people ready to sing His praises. I feel His quickening in my spirit. I forget my body, and suddenly I forget everything except why I am here—to tell His good news of deliverance to all who will listen.

Thirty years of arthritis and forty hospitalizations with surgeries for complications from this most severe form of the disease—none of that changes my calling. The worse my health becomes, the more tenacious I feel.

God has called me. He has seen me through desperate circumstances. I will never stop serving Him until He has used me up. That has been my lifelong vow.

As I sat in a service recently, I felt again within me the strength God has supplied so many times. My church deacons always see to it that I am settled in front of the congregation. They put me in whatever chair is best for me, so I can see everyone. Sometimes it is painful to get settled at first, but soon I forget everything except anticipation at the beginning of another opportunity to praise God in worship.

Sometimes visitors come to the church who used to know me long ago when I could walk and do everything everyone else can do. When they come, I want to tell them how gracious God has been to me. They don't see my tireless energy. At first they see only my frail frame, and they always notice my hands. Once I saw an old friend crying for me. She had not seen me in many years since her move away from Texas. I know I looked worse to her than at our last class reunion when I had still been able to stand on crutches. I've seen grown men cry as they remember me as their class leader and childhood friend: energetic and tireless in thinking up things for the rest of them to do. But I always feel that their eyes have deceived them. They don't see the energy God has placed within me.

I wish everyone could have been a part of my sixth anniversary service. My deacon, Brother A. C. Clark, said, "When you see Robert Gilbert, you have to remember something: he's not sick. When the Lord cured him, He fixed him that way!"

I remember we all laughed at the words, and some said a vigorous "Amen!" along with me. I'd never heard anyone put it quite like that before, but it's somehow true: the Lord "fixed me this way." And I know that He intends to keep me, just as He is faithful to everyone who truly seeks His strength. No situation—mental or physical—can keep us from serving God with all He intends for us.

I can still hear Brother Clark's words: "A leader is chosen by God, like Joseph or Moses—or Rev. Gilbert for this church.

"When someone asks me, 'How is Rev. Gilbert doing?' I say, 'Fine!'

"They say, 'Well, I just don't see how he does what he does.'

"And I say, 'Well, God fixed him this way so He could use him. Rev. Gilbert's not sick. It's impossible for a sick man to do what he does!'"

That's so true. For now, anyhow, I am certainly "fixed this way." God has allowed it.

But I know something else. Health is on the inside. Healing is on the inside. No matter what our circumstances, God can use us just as we are, if we put ourselves in His hands. I've been through many valleys and across many mountains to prove God's overwhelming grace and power.

Brother Clark, who said those words, knows what he is talking about. He has seen me at my worst. He visited me when I was so sick just last year. He saw me right after the round of serious and unexplained fevers began and again after I was home from being rushed to Houston for open-heart surgery. On the way, when I had that slight stroke so

I couldn't speak or recognize anybody, God could have chosen that moment to end my life and ministry. But He chose to sustain me and to fulfill His promises for my life and for this church. I know it was the prayer and fasting of so many standing with God that saw me through. God can get us through anything, as we trust Him and as friends who love us stand together with us in prayer.

My members and friends have seen me go through a lot of pain. They helped care for me, with the other members of the church, during those long weeks of recovery. So they know that I told the Lord, "Fix me, and I'll work for You." I think they know how tempted I was to give up this last time.

No matter how mature we are in the faith, we are not beyond feeling despair. But God is always strong enough to bring us back up. I was so far down for so many weeks, I thought I'd never be able to serve again. Since I lost the muscle tone in my legs, I can't be as physically active as I think I need to be. I haven't been able to drive a car. But even setbacks in my physical condition do not deter the Lord from working His own kind of recovery in my life, so I am His servant as much as I ever was.

Brother Clark told this story about my recovery:

"Rev. Gilbert thought he was on his way to heaven. He was one third of the way up the mountain when a man stood by him. It was Jesus, and He said to Rev. Gilbert, 'We're not ready for you yet. I'm gonna send you back to work!'"

"All right!" I said when he told that to everyone at my anniversary service. I laughed out loud when I first heard this story. All the people attending my service at Carver Park clapped.

Then the choir began singing: "Have you any mountains?" They knew my favorite songs were about mountains. I used to sing that mountains seem to flatten when you pray, in earlier days when I was well and strong. I used to sing it often at the old Antioch Baptist Church.

The song, in effect, told the mountain to get out of the way. I still think of that song when I awake in pain and think what I need to do for the Lord that day.

"Move, Mountain. Get out of my way!" Those are words very near the front of my mind.

I've seen God move mountains so many times. That is my testimony, every time I meet someone who wants to know why I have more joy than ever before. I'll never doubt the power of God. I declare:

Mountain, get out of my way.
That is what God did for me.
He fixed me so I could serve.

I've learned with Paul to hear God say, "My grace is sufficient for thee: for my strength is made perfect in weakness" (2 Cor. 12:9). I accept that today.

In fact, when I'm busy with the concerns of this church, the needs of these people, and the enabling of Jesus, I don't even think about myself. I don't know whether I feel good or bad, once I open my mouth to speak His Word. I forget everything except what He has given me to do.

I'm to the point where I don't bother the Lord anymore about my condition. I'm grateful for His sparing me some more time to be around. He has shown me how much He can do with so little of my physical strength.

When I pray with people and see His power at work to change their lives, I don't complain about needing anything more than I already have to serve with. If He can use me this way, I'm satisfied.

I want to wear out being used. I've said to the Lord, "Here, use me, until You use me up." I mean that.

My thoughts soared one Sunday night during evening services. I thought of all God has allowed me to do. Most of all, I recalled with thanks that I had a sound mind and a voice to speak His words.

A guest preacher, Rev. Lonnie Garrett, stood up in my church to speak. His sermon reminded me to be thankful for my voice: God's special instrument. "Sing the songs of Zion," he said. The idea excited me and I saw others listening expectantly.

"The children of Israel had trouble singing the songs of Zion in a strange land," he said.

"But Paul and Silas, when they were thrown in prison, began to sing after midnight, and their shackles fell off. They discovered they were free. Be able to sing in captivity or any other trouble. You never know when you'll need to sing. Have a song ready!"

The people were excited when Rev. Garrett finished, and so was I. I think we all wanted to burst into singing. The choir began to hum quietly for a while. Then the pianist played an introduction I recognized so well. I knew it was my turn.

Sunday after Sunday, as long as I had breath and strength, I had sung the same song to close out every service. My muscles may be weak, but my voice is still the voice of a strong man—a gift of God from my youth. At home I would often sing as my older sister, LaRue, played our old piano.

As soon as I could drag myself back to Carver Park to resume my services after my heart surgery, I began to sing this lifelong favorite again—louder and stronger every week.

If the people had closed their eyes, they could have imagined me a robust, athletic person with a barrel chest. That's

His Eye Is on the Sparrow: And I Know He Watches Me

how the sound always seemed when it came out: rounded and whole.

I began to sing the well-known verse; As it led into the chorus, a tremor of excitement swept through the people.

I heard their clapping now, so I began the chorus again, their amens rising with the words to "His Eye Is on the Sparrow."

The chorus of amens and clapping filled my ears as I held on to the last note.

I felt straight, free, and beyond pain. Jesus was in me and in that place.

My wife's hand lifted slightly toward me and toward heaven, then slid to her side. I saw her smile.

I felt the flush rise to my cheeks.

It was not the flush of fever. Not fever at all.

The Spirit of Christ had lifted me up to worship and praise. My soul was thanking God for strength to lift up my voice for Him.

The choir was clapping with my spirit, in praise to the Lord. Then they swirled down from the choir stands, marching one by one through the church aisles and out the door.

It is another Sunday morning and my mind is drifting to the sermon I am ready to preach—a message I want my church to understand as much as I want them to understand anything.

"Oh my people," I think, "will you seek and find the right way . . . the way that leads to everlasting life?"

My deacons come and lift me onto the high-backed stool where I sit to preach. I have been sitting in a motorized wheelchair which looks almost like a minibike—a recent gift from my congregation. But when I preach, I want to be able to see my people as I talk to them.

As I settle into the chair, I reach for my yellow lined paper with the sermon notes on it, and my deacon tucks the Bible into my lap. I won't need to consult it. I have studied several hours and prayed over this sermon. Besides, my eyesight keeps me from close reading during the service so my mind must be always clear about what I want to say.

My son Kenyatta appears at my side to wipe my face with his white handkerchief before I begin. The boys are doing more and more for me these days so my wife has to do less. I don't know sometimes what I would do without their help. They show an affection for me that brings tears to the eyes of those who watch them taking care of me. Of course they want to run and play, too, but they take their care for me seriously, especially while we are at church. One of the two of them is always close by. Ja Ja stands behind me often at the close of the service, waiting.

The church is quiet now, ready to hear what God has given me. I read to them the text for the day: "There is a way that seemeth right to a man. But the end thereof is the way of death" (Prov. 14:12).

"Yes, friends," I say. "There is a way that is moral, a way that seems to be the right way for us, even a way that religiously seems right to us. But none of those 'seeming ways' is enough. There is only one way for the Christian— the way that Christ tells us to follow . . . the *real* way.

"In the Bible, there is the right way, the wrong way, and the 'in-between' way. I think many of us are satisfied with the 'in-between' way. The in-between way *seems* right.

"But it is the wrong way. It is not the way of Christ.

"Let us never be satisfied with the in-between way. Let us only be satisfied with the way of Christ."

"I worry about people who think the majority way must be the right way. Why is that such a common belief? People say that 'everybody is doing it.' We seem to think the majority makes a thing all right.

"But did you know that the majority way may be the *wrong* way? In foreign policy, the war in Viet Nam 'seemed' to be right. The things we did in the Middle East 'seemed' to be the right way. But what do the results say today? Did these things only *seem* to be the right way?

"At home, we do things that "seem" right to us at the time, because we see everybody doing them. We have so many people living together outside of marriage because it 'seems' right, and 'everybody is doing it.' I ask you, does that make it right?

"People living together may decide to have a baby because it 'seems the right thing to do at the moment.' Besides, 'everybody we know is doing it,' they reason. But what will the results be?

"If we don't like the results, 'we can always have an abortion.' After all, 'everybody else is doing it.' It *seems* like the best way out.

"I am here to say that there are some things that *seem* to be right because the majority is doing them, but they are morally wrong.

"They may be legally all right, but they are morally wrong. In the sight of God, they are wrong.

"What about the drug scene? Everybody seems to be involved in drugs these days. At home, parents are taking alcohol, so the kids think it's the thing to do. We have to take our responsibility to our children seriously. We have to teach our young people the *right* way, and not expect the schools to do for our children what we cannot do for them ourselves.

"Even in religion, we have some ways that 'seem' right, but they may not be right at all. Some of the things we do are things that we excuse because 'Grandma did them this way' or because 'our denomination does it this way and our way is best.' But when we're relying on tradition, we may have all the form, all the prayers, all the weekly activities. But where has *real* religion gone?

"In our services we may feel a certain zeal, we may feel eager, emotional, or we may even shout when we feel good. But maybe we have a zeal that the Bible says is 'not according to knowledge.' "

"Sometimes God says to us to just 'be still and know that I am God.'

"What is the right way? Knowing God is what religion is all about. Only by knowing Him can we truly find the way that leads to life.

"What does Jesus say is the right way? It is a way that requires no excuses or apologies.

"When Jesus gave answers, He didn't say, 'This *seems* to be the right way.'

"He said, 'I am the Way.'

"At the Last Supper, Jesus said He was ready to go back to the Father, 'to prepare *the way* for you.' He said to them, 'The way *you know."* (John 14) He said He would show us *the way*.

"Thomas asked, 'How can we know the way?'

"Jesus answered Thomas, 'unless you come *by Me* . . . you will not find the way.'

"And to show the disciples that He truly was the Way, He died, was in the grave, and then He got up on Sunday morning!

"Yes," I hear my congregation saying to me at those words of good news. *Jesus got up on Sunday morning!*

I continue, "Jesus said before He left this earth, 'All power in heaven and earth is given unto Me.'

"Yes, Lord," the people say again in echo to my words.

I say, "Do you want to get closer to the Father? The only way is through Jesus Christ. Today, Jesus says, 'Come unto Me.'

"The door of the church and of heaven are open for you to come through it to the right Way.

"Some of you are tired of trying *'this way and that.'*

"Today, you have an invitation to come by the *only* Way—that Way is Jesus.

"Come now!

"If you ask Him, He will answer."

The choir begins to sing softly,

In the faces of so many I see the conviction of faith. I see the people saying within their hearts, "I know that's right!"

I know God will meet every need. He will, because He is the Way.

God's hand still seems powerful in my life as I seek to do even more for Him every day. I have vowed to stay in this church for as long as I have breath and strength. I have so many plans yet for this church—plans for the church to be a helping agency to all the poor and needy of our town, a band of believers who pour themselves out for others, a place where children can come and prepare themselves to be all God intends for them to be.

God has allowed me many dreams for this church. He has given me the tenacity and the commitment to wait upon Him for their realization. I know He can do far beyond all that we ask or think. He has done that abundantly in my life. He is doing that in this church.

I want everyone to know the power of God as I have experienced it. Nothing in this world—fear, depression, illness, weakness, suffering, rejection—can separate us from the love and care of Christ.

Without Him, I would have given up long ago. He alone has the strength to see us through.

An old preacher in my home church used to say to people who were having problems, "Tie a knot in the rope, and hold on!" I have done that by faith so many times. I have seen many others do it, too, holding on to a faithful God.

God is faithful. If we hold on, He will see us through. He has never failed me. He has never failed anyone who trusted in Him. I know today that He can do all things.

I know there is no excuse on earth I can make that will keep God from showing His power and His care for me. All I have to do is let go and wait upon Him. He is always ready to answer prayer and to sustain me—and anyone else—while we are waiting for His answers. Nothing in the world can separate us from His faithfulness and love.

I will never say, "I can't," as long as God shows Himself to me so faithfully. God alone is my life and my strength.

Each year I understand in a new way the words of Paul who said "I can do all things through Christ which strengtheneth me" (Phil. 4:13).

Yes, I can. God is able.

Amen.